Stephen Falconer Jones

Escape From Uxbridge

A working life in far-flung places

Mereo Books

2nd Floor, 6-8 Dyer Street, Cirencester, Gloucestershire, GL7 2PF
An imprint of Memoirs Books. www.mereobooks.com
and www.memoirsbooks.co.uk

Escape from Uxbridge

ISBN: 978-1-86151-974-0

First published in Great Britain in 2021
by Mereo Books, an imprint of Memoirs Books.

Copyright ©2021

The address for Memoirs Books can be found at www.mereobooks.com

Mereo Books Ltd. Reg. No. 12157152

Typeset in 11/15pt Century Schoolbook by Wiltshire Associates.
Printed and bound in Great Britain

CONTENTS

To my wife Lesley, my children Ben and Lara,
their spouses Victoria and Gavin,
and my grandchildren
Evie, Archie, Caleb and Eleanor

PREFACE

Among the multiple reasons for writing this memoir, first and foremost were selfish ones, to amuse myself and to dig deeper into the strange phenomenon of the wanderlust that engulfed me for so many years. Then there was the hope that my family might enjoy it, together with the pleasing mental image of my grandchildren reading my words when they are adults and I am long gone.

A wider audience might even find something of interest or amusement. Apart from a wish to record some experiences in various countries around the world, I also wanted to reflect on some of the lessons that might be learnt about the way the 'aid industry' worked in the 1970s, 80s and 90s. Not that I have any astonishing insights to offer about how development assistance to poor countries should be delivered, but I can point to some of the pitfalls and absurdities.

I have never counted the number of countries I have visited or worked in. Such an exercise would seem like showing off, akin to those executives in whose offices a wall map of the world is adorned with a flag for each country visited. The number of flags for me might be in the region of 70 or 80, but my aim has never been to tick off countries like the bus numbers I sadly used to collect as a small boy standing at the traffic lights in Uxbridge High Street. Instead it has been to experience the fascination of so many different and disparate places, none of which I regret visiting.

The wanderlust has ebbed over the years but not disappeared, and I look forward to further adventures.

CHAPTER 1

ESCAPE TO ZAMBIA, 1969/70

The seed was sown one day in 1963. *Please Please Me* by the Beatles was playing every night on Radio Luxembourg and the world was slowly getting over the shock of the assassination of John F Kennedy. A student teacher of Economics took a first-year 6th Form class at Bishopshalt Grammar School and happened to mention that a friend of his was going to Africa as a teacher working for an organisation called Voluntary Service Overseas (VSO).

Before that time it had not occurred to me that my horizons could extend very far beyond West London. Most people grew up, married and worked in the same place. People like me aspired to move up a rung on the social class ladder and perhaps own a semi-detached house in Ruislip. Few people, apart from the upper classes, had foreign holidays and even fewer travelled abroad to work. But things were changing. We were the first generation of kids from ordinary families, in large numbers, supported by government grants, to have the chance of going to university, providing a passport to mobility and, for those who wanted it, 'the world'.

The idea of becoming a VSO volunteer slowly took hold. It was met with some incredulity, but not hostility, by my parents. Their own foreign adventures had amounted to a long weekend in Paris for their honeymoon in 1936 and they had neither the ambition, nor the money, to go abroad again. In spite of living a few miles from London Airport, not renamed Heathrow until 1966, neither of my parents ever flew in an aeroplane in their entire lives and were not at all dismayed by this omission. They viewed my plan as dangerous, foolhardy and totally outside their own experience, but put no obstacles in my way.

In August 1969, after 'A' levels, a year of working to earn some money and three years at Exeter University, armed with a middling degree, and having successfully passed a fairly rigorous VSO recruitment process, I was informed of my posting to Mungwi Secondary School in Northern Province of Zambia, where I was to teach whatever I was asked to teach.

My motivation was first and foremost to travel and have some adventures, but I also had a strong wish to 'do something useful'. This was the era of African countries extracting their independence from Britain. Mau Mau in Kenya was a receding memory, regrettably Ian Smith had declared UDI (Unilateral Declaration of Independence) in Rhodesia in 1965, but elsewhere, leaders such as Nkrumah, Nyerere, Kenyatta and Kaunda were in charge of independent countries. It was a genuinely exciting period and chimed well with my left-wing leanings at the time. In spite of great problems there was real hope that a bright new era was dawning in Africa, and I was greatly enthused to be playing a small part in it.

Thus began my journey of doing development work in Third World countries which would occupy me for much of the next 30 years, providing many adventures and many highs and lows, but also frequent bouts of frustration and disappointment to counterbalance the occasional feelings of achievement and satisfaction.

BOAC flight 51 to Lusaka took off from Heathrow on the 6th September 1969, my first long-haul journey, ticket price £78 and 4 shillings, with stops, including disembarkation, at Cairo and Nairobi. After all those years of living near the airport and wishing I was on board the planes I could see departing for exotic foreign parts, I was now on one. Sleep was impossible due to the level of excitement and expectation. The flight was enormously enjoyable, even the food, and this was palpably the beginning of the rest of my life.

People often talk of 'culture shock' when visiting a distant part of the world for the first time, but I was not aware of any such feelings on my arrival in Lusaka. It was a big, noisy, smelly city, but not very different from what I expected. Of course there were all sorts of discoveries and surprises. We experienced jacaranda, frangipani and hummingbirds for the first time. A few of my fellow volunteers were very taken aback by a headline in *The Times of Zambia* shortly after our arrival which read 'Woman has clitoris cut out in the Copperbelt', but the surprises were fewer than we might have expected and our group of about a dozen fresh-faced volunteers, mostly just out of university, soon adapted to our new situation.

First impressions of Lusaka were quite favourable except for the shanty towns on the outskirts, but the centre was surprisingly modern and people were friendly. We explored the sights in and around Cairo Road, the main street, named after Cecil Rhodes' dream of a British Empire extending from Cape Town to Cairo, with Lusaka being about one-third of the way up the continent.

My previous travel experience had only extended to hitch-hiking round a few countries in Western Europe, but Africa did not feel as alien as friends and relatives in England had predicted. Perhaps my background reading, along with the VSO induction courses and my growing interest in African politics, had prepared me reasonably well. We knew we were not going to a country where people wore loin cloths and bones through their noses. Short-sleeved shirts and cotton trousers, admittedly often very threadbare, were much more the order of the day. This was not the Africa of famines and war, just a poor country, populated predominantly by subsistence farmers and their families, getting on with life. In fact, the population at this time was only 4 million (compared to 16 million in 2015 at the time of my most recent visit) spread thinly around a land area almost as large as the UK and France combined.

Even when I flew up to Kasama, the capital of Northern Province, some 600 miles from Lusaka, in an old Dakota plane which had reportedly been used by Jan Smuts in the Second World War, the experiences were still broadly within the realms of expectation. The journey from Kasama to the village of Mungwi was about 25 miles down a red laterite road (the only tarmac within 200 miles was a short stretch in the middle of town), past giant termite mounds and then left at the 'elephant and castle', a junction marked by an elephant skull and a hoarding for the ubiquitous Castle Beer.

Of course there were surprises from time to time, some of which were pleasant rather than unpleasant. Prior to my departure I had imagined living in a mud hut, but I found myself living in a better standard of accommodation than I had ever previously experienced. Having come from a council-owned flat over some shops in Uxbridge High Street, I now shared a pleasant three-bedroomed bungalow on the school campus, supplied with electricity and running water, except when the pump at the local dam failed.

Some surprises were language based. English was the lingua franca, but particular forms of Zambian usage had developed. Nobody batted an eyelid at assembly on my first school morning when the headmaster, Mr Mulenga, announced 'the Land Rover is buggered', because that word had simply come to mean 'broken'.

Another pleasant surprise was that the climate was delightful. In later years I made a number of work visits to Nigeria and Sierra Leone in West Africa and sweltered in horrible, humid heat but here in this part of Zambia, on a flat plateau at about 5,000 feet above sea level, the temperature seldom got uncomfortably hot and even the wet season was quite bearable, apart from the dirt roads turning into quagmires.

There were so few secondary schools in Zambia at the time that many of them were required to be boarding schools in order to cater for children who lived at great distances. About 600 boys were boarders at Mungwi Secondary School, and they were the lucky ones. Most Zambian kids received some primary level education, but only those who both passed the exams and had parents who could afford the modest school fees and uniform costs proceeded to the secondary level. There was another weeding-out process after two years, when the 'Form 2' exams were taken. The very lucky few in Forms 3, 4 and 5 went on to take Cambridge 'O' Level, which, if passed, provided a passport directly to university or a good job.

Zambia's main natural resource, then as now, was copper, and the ambition of most boys was to get a cushy office job working for one of the mining companies, such as Anglo-American, in one of the Copperbelt towns such as Ndola. Those who left school after Form 2, either because of exam failure or lack of funds, also aspired to clerical work or, strange as it may sound with such a meagre level of educational attainment, they could gain entry to teacher training courses. The great need in Zambia was for educated youngsters to work in the agriculture and food sector, but even though Agricultural Science was taught at Mungwi in conjunction with a sizable school farm, farming was associated in the minds of the pupils with the subsistence lifestyle of most of their parents and they simply did not want to 'get their hands dirty'.

At the time of independence in 1964, when Northern Rhodesia became Zambia, the country had only a handful of doctors, engineers and others with essential professional qualifications. The British colonial legacy was not a proud one in this regard. There were few Zambian teachers who were fully qualified to teach at secondary level. Hence, when I arrived at Mungwi, there were only two Zambian teachers at the school out of a staff of more than 20. One of those two was a fascinating character who had been so determined to obtain a secondary education when he was a teenager that he had walked to Uganda, where he had been befriended by an English couple and had ended up having his secondary education in Walsall before returning to Zambia as a teacher to help other kids get the locally-based education that he had been denied.

The second Zambian teacher, as was the usual and understandable practice, was promoted to be headmaster. Mr Mulenga was an intelligent and capable head teacher who was prone to giving miscreant boys rather severe beatings, as was the norm at the time, and he also had a tendency to go missing for days on end leaving his long-suffering deputy, Mr Patel, in charge. Like many Zambians, Mr Mulenga was very fond of beer. Excessive drinking was an enormous problem for the nation as a whole and among the consequences was that Zambia had one of the highest rates of death on the roads due to drink-driving. The railway company even introduced breathalyser tests for train drivers because so many trains got derailed or just came to a stop in the middle of nowhere.

The other teachers at the school constituted a mini United Nations of nationalities. Most were contract teachers funded out of the aid budgets of their respective countries, a few were volunteers and some were on commercial contracts paid by the Zambian Government, which was enjoying the proceeds of high copper prices at the time. The deputy headmaster was from India, two teachers were East African Asians, three came from the Soviet Union, two from Canada, one from New Zealand, one American (a gentle giant, former professional basketball player who was reputedly funded by a black power group although I never saw any evidence of that), two from Northern Ireland, one from Scotland and several from England, including one of Asian origin. Most were hard-working and highly professional teachers who signed up to the collective goal of giving our students an excellent start in life.

I sometimes wonder if this was a golden age for the Zambian education system, because within the next decade or so, most of the foreign teachers were replaced by Zambian nationals, many of whom were poorly trained and poorly remunerated, particularly after government revenues slumped when the world market price for copper fell dramatically. Obviously it was unsustainable and undesirable for most teachers in Zambia to be foreigners, but during that brief window of time the students certainly benefited from high standards.

Not that there weren't some disadvantages to having teachers from so many countries. One of the difficulties faced by the students was trying to disentangle the mangled English of some of the teachers and the great variety of accents, remembering also that English was the second, or sometimes third, language of the students themselves. Most difficult was Pete Paschenko. He had worked as a Maths teacher in various parts of Africa for many years, but he had his own very eccentric version of English which was made more difficult to understand by the fact that he invariably had a Rothmans in his mouth.

The Russians had quite a big presence in Zambia in this period, not only teachers but other professions as well. All our doctors in the local town of Kasama were Russians, with a reputation for being rather knife happy. Although we were all aware of Cold War tactics being acted out in Africa, relationships among the teachers at the school were very harmonious and we all celebrated each other's national holidays. A lot of vodka flowed every May 1st.

The ever-present and hard-working Mr Patel provided complications on a couple of fronts. One was that Mr Danta, a science teacher, was higher caste than Mr Patel and Mr Danta's mother, who lived with him on the school campus, forbade her son to share the same food table as Mr Patel, even when we were all present at a school function. Another difficulty was Mr Patel's heavily accented English, which sometimes stumped the staff as well as the students. On one of the many occasions when Mr Patel was standing in for the head and leading the morning assembly, held every day at 7am in the open air, he railed against the practice of 'wishering' by some students. He went on about this at some length, making 'wishering' seem really quite serious. Afterwards, the staff debated what this particular sin might be and after being questioned by the students on the same subject, someone plucked up courage to ask the man himself for an explanation. It turned out that the sin was whistling.

I was 22 years old and some of the students were older than me. The difficulties of passing exams, raising some money and being spared from working on the family plot of land meant that there were often big gaps in an individual's education and some might still be doing their 'O' levels when approaching, or even over, 20 years old.

In spite of the advanced age of some students, discipline at the school was quite good, even though some class sizes were in excess of 40, even 50 in the case of evening classes composed of local young men and women who were still trying to pass their Form 2 exams. The only time there was a complete breakdown of discipline was over food riots by the boarders. The main diet for the boys was *nshima* (mealie meal made from maize flour) with *kapenta* (a small sardine-like fish from Lake Tanganyika). It was a very repetitive and boring diet and sometimes the deliveries were late. On one occasion the rioters started burning school buildings. The headmaster was absent and most staff decided to beat a strategic retreat to the local town for a few hours, but Mr Patel refused to go, with the words 'I will die here if necessary'.

Fortunately, no one died; the local paramilitary troops restored order by lining up the boys on the school field and took pleasure in dishing out beatings to those they felt were getting a better education than they themselves had received.

The subjects I taught were English (Form 2), History ('O' level), Civics (Form 2) and Geography at night school. The syllabuses left a lot to be desired in terms of relevance to people living in the middle of the African continent at a time of historic change. The history syllabus focused on 19th century Europe, Italian unification and all that. The geography syllabus was not much better and I still have a vivid memory of my first week in the job, trying to explain the Labrador Current and its influence on the climate of Newfoundland while a young woman placated a crying child by breast feeding. Common practice in Africa, but a surprise the first time it happened in one of my classes.

The subject of Civics was taken by all students in the first two years of secondary school. It had a surprisingly good syllabus, relevant to all young Zambians, consisting of basic information about the political and economic life of the country. All was well until one day when I had been following the syllabus in a particular class, extolling the virtues of the multi-party system, when later in the day news filtered through on the radio that President Kaunda, like so many other African leaders, had announced his intention to declare a one-party state and the one party was his own, UNIP. A number of tricky questions followed in class the next day, but the syllabus would take time to change and multi-party democracy was still the order of the day in the exams which followed shortly afterwards, leading one bright spark memorably to write, bearing in mind that many Africans confuse the letters L and R in the same way as the Japanese, that 'the President holds an erection once every five years'. Furthermore, 'in between general erections he holds by-erections'. (In a similar vein *The Times of Zambia*, some years later, reported that a speaker at a conference 'was greeted with sustained crapping'.)

Apart from occasional problems such as the food riots, it was a happy time and I well remember the feeling of elation, not experienced in later working life, of walking away from a lesson when I really felt that I had successfully imparted some important knowledge to the class. I also had a feeling of deep satisfaction when the Form 2 and 'O' level exam results were received, showing a high level of good passes. On completion of my VSO contract, I left Zambia with the feeling that I had discharged my responsibilities to the students because, although there is more to education than exam results, that was the sole measure of success in their eyes.

A few years later I began a career as an agricultural economist, working firstly for the British aid programme and then for a private consultancy company working on contracts for agencies such as the World Bank, United Nations and European Union, sometimes in Africa but also in other parts of the world. Many of the feasibility studies and other planning missions resulted only in reports gathering dust on shelves. Those projects that did see the light of day sometimes foundered due to corruption, conflict and incompetence on the part of host governments. It was not all doom and gloom and there were shining examples of good practice and successful projects from time to time. However, I sometimes wonder if my most useful contribution over a 30-year career was actually spent as a novice teacher in a remote part of central Africa rather than as a so-called 'expert' working for most of the highfaluting aid agencies.

CHAPTER 2

SIDE TRIPS, 1969/70

A white Christmas in South Africa

'You've come for a white Christmas' smirked the border guard in a thick South African accent when he saw the Zambian resident stamp in my passport. The date was 16th December, 1969 and the place was the Limpopo River border crossing at Beitbridge between Rhodesia and South Africa.

Like many people I met on this trip, the border guard assumed that life must be hell in 'black' Africa and any person of European descent must be falling over themselves to spend some time in the 'civilisation' of apartheid South Africa. Nothing could be further from the truth as far as I was concerned, but I kept my mouth firmly shut for fear of being denied entry to the country if I displayed my true colours.

'Would you like a lift to Cape Town?' Edie had asked in her broad Belfast accent a few weeks previously. Such a question would have been perfectly sensible if the conversation had taken place somewhere in Cape Province, but we were 1,800 miles away as the crow flies and an awful lot further by road. It transpired that Edie and her husband, both teachers at the school, planned to spend Christmas with friends in South Africa and they were willing to take me so long as I clearly understood that I would be offloaded in Cape Town and then make my own way back, a round trip of over 5,000 miles.

This presented me with a dilemma. It was a fantastic offer with the prospect of adventure, wonderful scenery and visiting fascinating places that I had only ever dreamt of seeing, but VSO had decreed that volunteers should not visit Rhodesia or South Africa because of UDI and apartheid respectively. Also, I was required to attend a VSO training course in Lusaka in early January. A plan started to take shape in my mind, because it was unthinkable that I could pass up this opportunity. I would accept the offer, then hitchhike from Cape Town to Lusaka via Durban, Johannesburg, Bulawayo and the Victoria Falls, arriving just in time for the course so that no one would be any the wiser about where I had been. With the optimism of youth I completely overlooked the risks inherent in this plan.

We set off at 5am on a dark December morning in Edie and Jeff's Toyota station wagon, as such cars were called in those days, even before the strong smell of wood smoke started emerging from the mud huts in the local villages. Five days later we arrived at our destination. The first 100 miles were driven on dirt roads, then nearly all the remainder of the journey on tarmac roads, sometimes strip tarmac where you drove down the strip when there was nothing coming in the opposite direction but then moved over with two tyres off the tarmac to accommodate oncoming vehicles, hoping that they would do the same thing.

The first overnight stop was at the house of friends in Kitwe on the Zambian Copperbelt, a total transformation from tiny, rural, agricultural, friendly Mungwi. Surrounded by copper mines, factories and large housing estates, we were now among expatriates whose main topic of conversation was the high crime rate, to the extent that it was not uncommon for them to put chains round the axles of their cars at night to prevent them being stolen. In Mungwi, my housemate and I never possessed a key to our house and would go away on holiday just shutting the door behind us, safe in the knowledge that robbery was virtually unknown.

The second overnight stay, after crossing into Ian Smith's illegally independent Rhodesia, was in the capital, Salisbury, not renamed Harare until legal independence in 1980. This was a place seemingly modelled on pleasant towns in Surrey and it was difficult to believe that you were actually in Mashonaland. The guerrilla war against white minority rule had not yet intensified and there were no restrictions on travel, at least not if you were white.

After crossing the Limpopo, the remaining two and a half days were spent traversing the vast expanse of South Africa with fascinating and ever-changing scenery ranging from large urban areas, with diamond and gold mines, to near desert (the Great Karoo) and the mountains and fertile parts of Cape Province.

A sinking yet excited feeling gripped me as I watched Edie and Jeff's car pull away after dropping me off in a street in central Cape Town with a cheery 'have fun – see you back in Mungwi'. 'What have I done?' I thought to myself as I considered how little money I had and what a long way back it was. Never mind, Cape Town soon beguiles you. The setting is sensational; of all the cities I have visited in the world, it is only beaten by Rio de Janeiro. There was Table Mountain, invariably with a layer of cloud on top known as the table cloth, the Cape of Good Hope, whale watching, people watching, and particularly the intriguing mix of races, none more mixed than the Cape Coloureds, as they were known at the time, who constituted about 10% of the total population of the country.

My trip up Table Mountain was in danger of being cancelled due to the high winds that had nearly blown me off my feet the previous day, but the wind abated sufficiently for the cable car to recommence its service. While in the queue to buy my ticket, an elderly lady addressed a remark to me in Afrikaans. I apologised that I did not speak the language and was taken aback by a barrage of invective, delivered in English, that I should be ashamed of myself for not being bilingual. The awful Boer War had been over for nearly 70 years by this time, but old hatreds seemed not too far from the surface. Even when I explained that I was a tourist from England, she only scowled and made no attempt to apologise.

After a few days, knowing that time pressure was upon me, I took a bus ride to the outskirts of Cape Town and started waving my thumb in the air. I had been told that a white male with short hair, looking reasonably smart (clean shorts and shirt), stood the best chance of getting lifts. And so it turned out. Sporting my new haircut, I soon got my first lift and I was on my way down the famous Garden Route towards Port Elizabeth and East London. With the Drakensberg Mountains to my left and occasional views of the coast to my right, I sped through this beautiful country, reaching Durban in time to spend Christmas Day getting sunburnt on the beach – a very strange experience for a little-travelled Englishman.

Hitchhiking turned out to be an effective way of getting around, albeit with some odd experiences. On one occasion, I had been waiting for an hour or more on the edge of a small town and was getting anxious as dusk fell and still no lift was forthcoming until a car travelling at considerable speed braked sharply and reversed with tyres spinning to where I was standing. Instead of the usual question of 'where are you going', I was faced with 'can you drive?' My affirmative answer was greeted by the young South African with some relief as he got out of the driving seat and then lay down in the back of the car. It turned out that he had been on the road continuously for the past 12 hours and had an important appointment the next morning. Without further ado he fell soundly asleep, seemingly unconcerned that I might be a thief or murderer, while I drove all night, arriving at our destination in time for breakfast.

All my lifts in South Africa were given by white people, with one exception. I was hitchhiking on a road north of Pretoria when to my surprise an old beaten-up VW van pulled up alongside. The driver, an African gentleman with a great big smile on his face, indicated that I should slide back the door on the side of the van, which I did, revealing a large family, all sitting on the floor and all smiling broadly. There was a great deal of squeezing up and excited chatter, until a small space was cleared just sufficient for my six foot two inch frame to sit cross-legged. We set off, going goodness knows where, because nobody spoke a word of English. After some time, the van drew to a halt and gesticulations indicated that it was time for me to get out. I found myself standing on a long, straight, empty road with nothing in sight except a sign saying, 'Tropic of Capricorn'. After giving me a cheery goodbye wave, the driver did a U-turn and the van slowly disappeared down the road we had come along, leaving me totally bemused as to why this charming family had thought I wanted to stand in the middle of nowhere, with one foot in the tropics.

Travel in South Africa in December 1969 for a young white man travelling alone was not dangerous, in stark contrast to later years. I hated being called 'boss', but I did take advantage of apartheid to the extent of enjoying safe travel. In a letter home to my parents I wrote 'for scenery and climate South Africa is absolutely fantastic, and in different political circumstances it could be a paradise on earth. The journey reaffirmed my opinions about apartheid, which is a nauseating and inefficient system. Quite simply it doesn't work – it's impossible to separate the races'.

Whites and non-whites had different entrances to shops, different public telephone boxes, different park benches, different beaches and so on. The stupidity of the system was reinforced to me when I witnessed a white lady knocked down on a zebra crossing. A passing non-white ambulance was not allowed to pick her up and she had to wait 20 minutes for a white ambulance to arrive.

I met many friendly and hospitable people during my stay, some with surprisingly liberal views, but there was general incredulity that any white person would voluntarily live in Zambia or any other independent African country. I was asked on more than one occasion 'do you sleep with a gun under your pillow?'

A close encounter on the road to Mpika

It is not uncommon to see children bowling hoops along the road in Zambia. This particular road was the Great North Road, previously known as the 'Hell Run' to Tanzania.

We first saw two tiny specks on the road in the far distance in the great emptiness that characterises this part of Zambia or it did then, in 1970. As we drew closer, we could see that they were boys. Derek's VW Beetle was eating up the miles and we still had over 200 miles to go on our way back to start the new term at Mungwi Secondary School where we were both teachers. Perhaps he should have slowed down more, but he did not realise that they were playing a game of dare. The boys for their part did not realise that the car would overtake them on the right rather than the left, and when they shot off to the right they both hit the car with great force. One boy hit my passenger side door, I saw his bony elbow and arm up against the glass for what seemed like seconds, and the other boy hit the rear wing.

People always said 'if you have an accident, whatever you do don't stop'. Only a few days previously in Lusaka, I had seen a driver knock over a pedestrian and the crowd quickly dragged him from his car and beat him up. That's just what happened.

Derek stopped the car and we looked back to see two seemingly lifeless figures in the centre of the road with their hoops still rolling before tipping over. We took it for granted that we had to get out and do something.

Both boys were about 10 years old, wearing cheap khaki shorts and shirts with no shoes. The first boy was bleeding profusely from the top of his head. His scalp was hanging off like a giant flap, semi-detached from his head. I left him for dead and went over to the second boy, who was beginning to stir. His most obvious injury was a badly broken leg.

As if by magic, a few people, perhaps ten, mostly men, emerged from the elephant grass at the side of the road. We had been totally unaware that there was anyone in the vicinity, but it was typical of the African bush that a small crowd could emerge out of nowhere.

One man said that he was the boys' uncle and that we must take them to Mpika hospital, which was about 20 miles away. In Europe or even in Lusaka one might have thought of telephoning for an ambulance, but such a thought was ridiculous in these circumstances. Therefore, the uncle's demand was entirely reasonable, except that the car was full of luggage and provisions. The uncle insisted on going with the boys, both of whom were now conscious but with awful injuries and crying and moaning loudly.

Derek and I were being swept along by events and were no longer in a decision-making position. The car was unloaded, the uncle was kneeling on the front seat, facing backwards, trying to comfort the boys who had been placed as carefully as possible on the back seat. With Derek as driver, the Beetle was full, leaving me, the luggage, provisions and a very large laundry basket, bought by Derek in Lusaka, at the side of the road.

Only as the car disappeared into the heat haze on the horizon did I start to take stock of my situation. The villagers were engaged in a whispered debate with lots of looks, not friendly ones, in my direction. For the first time I noticed that some of the men were carrying pangas, not surprising since these were commonly used on the farms and for cutting back the bush.

All this time there had been no traffic on the road, but now I saw a truck approaching in the distance. It was going in the wrong direction, but by this stage I just wanted to get the hell out of there. I stood in the middle of the road and flagged him down. Using sign language, I was making some progress in persuading the driver to take me when one of the villagers spoke curtly to him in Chibemba. My hopes sank as he accelerated away.

Meanwhile, Derek's mercy dash to the hospital had been accomplished and he had driven to the nearby police station.

The officer behind the desk took little interest until he got to the part about leaving me at the side of the road. 'What, you left a *musungu* (white man) at the scene?' In no time two Land Rovers stuffed full of police and Derek sped down the road. Finding only a great deal of blood and no sign of me, the police made an extensive search of the nearby bush to find my body, but gave up when darkness fell.

Fortunately for me, the next vehicle to pass the rather strange looking hitchhiker with a great deal of luggage was a local government official from Mungwi village who knew me. As we drove away in his old Mercedes he confirmed that some of the villagers had wanted to take the law into their own hands. He drove me to the hospital and then to the police station, where I waited for a couple of hours for the return of the search party. Only then did Derek realise that he would not need the letters he had mentally prepared to my parents and the British High Commissioner to report my death.

Opinions varied in the following weeks and months between those people, mostly women, who thought we were very brave and others, mostly men, who thought we were extremely stupid. The two boys recovered and the one with the head injury almost certainly would have died from loss of blood if we had not stopped. But the killer question was 'would you do the same thing again?' I don't know the answer to that.

Highway robbery in the Congo Pedicle

A line of ragtag soldiers was strung out across the pot-holed bush road with their rifles pointing directly at us. Conventional wisdom had it that these brigands had no bullets and were just trying their luck on the unsuspecting motorists crossing from one part of Zambia to another. The Congo Pedicle road offered a shortcut through 50 miles of bandit-ridden territory instead of a journey of hundreds of miles by staying on the safer routes inside Zambia.

Conventional wisdom is all well and good until you find yourself staring down the barrels of several guns. 'Just keep driving straight at them' advised the regular users of the road we met at the Zambia/Congo border post 'and they will scarper'.

Angus was driving. There was only about 50 yards of red laterite between us and them. We had a couple of seconds to make a decision, and we were trying to remain calm, weighing up the pros and cons of different reactions, but really in a blind panic.

This was not the first time we had faced danger on this journey which had started at the school where we were both teachers. We travelled down almost the full length of scenically beautiful Malawi, crossed into war-torn Mozambique, then into Rhodesia as it then was, back into Zambia and onward northwards via the Copperbelt, a round trip of about 2,000 miles, all undertaken in the most unsuitable of vehicles.

Whatever possessed Angus to buy a tiny Honda van when he first arrived in Zambia I will never know. Cheapness no doubt, but it was the sort of vehicle that might just have survived for a year or two on the tarmac roads of Lusaka but was spectacularly unsuited to the pot-holed, corrugated, dirt roads where we lived. Never mind all that. When Angus asked me if I would like to accompany him on a jaunt round Central Africa in the Easter holidays of 1970, I accepted with alacrity.

The Malawian border was only about 100 miles to the west of Mungwi. With the exception of the magnificent Victoria

Falls, Zambia's claims to scenic fame are few and far between, as the country is mostly flat plateau, but Malawi by contrast, from the Nyika Plateau in the north to Mulanje Mountain in the south, skirting the long, thin, beautiful Lake Malawi, is a travel brochure writer's dream. It is also desperately poor and had a very low standard of roads.

Our many adventures and mishaps included the Honda van's exhaust pipe parting company with the rest of the vehicle as we approached the lodge at Nyika Plateau, to the west of Lake Malawi, as night fell. A bad enough situation at the best of times, but the memory of trying to reattach a hot pipe in a game reserve with the sound of wild animals in my ears as I lay, exposed, under the vehicle, still gives me shivers.

From the south of Malawi we needed to traverse more than 100 miles of north-western Mozambique to reach the Rhodesian border. Crossing the vastly wide Zambesi River, close to the town of Tete, on a steel raft pulled by a boat of a similar age and state of dilapidation to the African Queen was always likely to be our most dangerous exploit in Mozambique, except that it wasn't. The previous day, on leaving the border with Malawi, I casually asked Angus if he knew which side of the road to drive on. 'Search me' he volunteered helpfully, 'all the old British colonies drive on the left but not sure about the Portuguese ones'.

The road was empty at this stage, but we stupidly agreed that I would drive down the middle until we saw an approaching vehicle. The only trouble was that the next one was a massive truck, itself trundling down the centre of the road, which would have wiped us out if I hadn't taken an instant decision to follow continental practice and drive on the right.

African travel at this time was greatly affected by local politics in the various countries. We lived under the fairly benign leadership of President Kenneth Kaunda in Zambia. This trip reminded us that Zambia was a relatively peaceful haven surrounded by more volatile countries. Crossing into Malawi, which was under the control of President for Life Hastings Kamuzu Banda, who liked to be referred to as 'Ngwazi' (Conqueror), we were soon reminded that this was a more repressive regime when stopped at a road block manned by Young Pioneers, menacing teenagers armed with guns who owed their allegiance to Banda.

The FRELIMO freedom fighters in Mozambique were still fighting their war of liberation and the country did not become independent until 1975. In Rhodesia, Ian Smith had declared UDI and Zimbabwe would not emerge as an independent country for another 10 years. As we crossed the border at the magnificent Kariba Dam, the sound of occasional gunfire being exchanged between the Zambian and Rhodesian forces was a reminder of the tensions between the two countries.

In the Congo, secessionist forces under Moise Tshombe in the early 1960s had tried to make the southern province of Katanga a separate state, but they had been defeated by the national forces under the ruthless President Mobutu Sese Seko. Some of Tshombe's former troops were still drifting around many years later, and no doubt we were looking at half a dozen of them through the windscreen.

'Accelerate!' I yelled as we sped towards possible oblivion. We both ducked down below the height of the dashboard and bumped heads painfully as the tiny car sped forwards. I was the first to look up, and I saw the trunk of an enormous banyan tree looming a few feet in front of us. Reaching across, I yanked

24

the steering wheel to the left and we screeched back onto the road, only just managing to avoid rolling over. We looked back and saw our intended robbers waving their fists at us in cartoon comedy fashion.

While delayed for some time at the Chembe Ferry border post, waiting to cross back into Zambia, we met the occupants of the next car behind us. They had stopped, and were robbed of all their valuables plus passports and other papers.

Angus and I felt a little bit brave and a little bit smug.

CHAPTER 3

HOMEWARD BOUND, 1971

Nearing completion of the four teaching terms of my VSO contract, decision time was approaching; whether to fly home from Zambia to London, with an estimated journey time of less than one day, or to travel overland and by sea, taking about three months. This was the choice confronting me as the close of the school term approached in December. VSO would make the arrangements for my flight if I chose that option, or they would pay me the equivalent of the fare, leaving me, somewhat nervously, on my own to organise the journey home.

I wrestled with the pros and cons. It would be lovely to see friends and family back in England, but an opportunity to travel halfway around the world might never present itself again. A possible route had already taken shape in my mind involving bus travel from Zambia, through Tanzania, to Mombasa in Kenya, followed by a sea crossing to Bombay, then steam train to Delhi to pick up the 'hippy trail' overland to Europe. In those halcyon days before wars and international strife closed borders it was entirely possible to plan a journey from India, through Pakistan, Afghanistan, Iran, Turkey, Greece and onwards to western Europe. Unlike today, it was then the 15 republics of the Soviet Union which presented the overland traveller with closed borders, or at least entry visa systems too awful to contemplate.

I remember lying awake one night mulling over the relative merits of the short, sharp and safe option against the great unknowns and possible hazards of the intrepid option and deciding the latter far outweighed the former. Having made that decision, there remained the little question of how to finance this journey. Money was in very short supply. VSO teachers are only paid pocket money and there was no possibility of a family loan being available. The Ministry of Education partly came to my rescue by making me head examiner for Form 2 Civics examinations in Northern Province. This meant delaying my departure, but I was well qualified for the task and it paid well. The remainder of the money I needed arrived courtesy of Mr Singh, a teacher at the same school, who was desperate to build up his savings in pounds sterling but was prevented from doing so by Zambian exchange control regulations. The deal was that I would repay the loan into his UK bank account on my return, after I had found some temporary employment, and he would trust me, albeit highly fretfully, to keep my side of the bargain.

It took some time for these financial arrangements to fall into place, but eventually I had enough to travel on a shoestring basis. The next question was whether or not to travel alone. Another teacher at the school briefly toyed with the idea of joining me, as did a Canadian nurse at the local hospital, an altogether more enticing prospect on one level, but they both thought better of it and I was left to my own devices. In retrospect that was far and away the best thing, because the possibility of tensions arising during such a long and complicated trip would have been extremely high, made worse by a requirement to act as a knight errant by not separating from a female companion in some godforsaken place after a row about where to go next. Much better to travel alone. As it happened, throughout the three months there were many occasions when I linked up with another traveller or travellers where it worked to our mutual advantage and then happily went our separate ways when our paths diverged.

Making the necessary travel arrangements in advance of my departure provided quite a challenge, as the only means of communication at my disposal was by post. Average time for an air mail letter to reach me from the UK was 10 days. Contrast this with a trip I made from England to Zambia in October 2015 when all the bookings were made online having previously checked timetables on the various airlines' websites and hotel reservations were confirmed after sifting through reviews on TripAdvisor and similar sites. Of course, none of this was available in 1970 and being based in a rural school in the backwoods of Zambia, I didn't even have access to a working telephone, certainly not one capable of making a call beyond a radius of about 25 miles. Today's young people with ready access to email, the Internet, Google, social media, mobile phones and much more find it virtually incomprehensible that a time existed, only a few decades ago, when none of this was invented. Even more surprising to them is that some other methods of communication, such as telex and fax, have come and gone in the meantime.

Consequently, I was at the mercy of the Zambian postal system. From previous trips to East Africa I knew that the shipping line that operated a service to Bombay from Mombasa was the wonderfully named 'British India Steam Navigation Company', and after an exchange of letters with the agent in Mombasa my passage on the eight-day crossing was booked. My equivalent of Google was a letter to my long-suffering dad in Uxbridge asking him to check which companies provided bus journeys on the 'hippy trail' starting in India. After some research, he informed me that 'P. Beesley (Kingston) Ltd' ran a regular service and I could catch a bus in Delhi on 6th February 1971 that would (theoretically) deliver me to London, 50 days later, if I paid the fare of £60. My Dad, bless him, paid the deposit of £15 and I was to pay the balance on arrival in Delhi.

Ease of communication got no better even after I left Zambia. The usual method of receiving mail for travellers like myself was to use the *poste restante* facility at large post offices in towns and cities around the world. Goodness knows how the staff ever managed to find anything in the dusty corners of these chaotic buildings, but the system sometimes worked tolerably well, although many letters went astray. International telephone calls were out of the question for cost reasons, unless there was a dire emergency, and thankfully that never happened. *Poste restante* was all that was left and even that failed the test due to an extended British postal workers' strike, which meant that no letters could be sent or received during my travels from India to Greece. Consequently, my family heard nothing from me for a period of six weeks. Only after I became a parent myself and my children started travelling the world, often with a mobile phone in their pockets that could call home from remote locations, did it occur to me what a nightmare of worry my parents must have endured.

My journey proper began on 29th December after spending Christmas with friends at Mbala, close to the southern shore of Lake Tanganyika, and they kindly drove me to the Zambia/Tanzania border at Tunduma, which was not much more than a truck stop on the Great North Road. I crossed the border on foot and for the first time contemplated the fact, with a mixture of exhilaration and trepidation, that I was now entirely on my own with a long, long way to travel on a very limited budget. It then took six hours to cover the 70 miles to Mbeya in the beautiful hills of that part of Tanzania owing to the road, and its many diversions, being turned into a quagmire by construction traffic transforming a dangerous dirt road into a tarmac highway but with utter chaos for bus travellers like myself in the meantime. At least I was now on my way.

Almost immediately outline travel plans had to be torn up and amendments made. Bus timetables in this part of Africa were usually works of complete fiction, partly due to the dreadful maintenance of antiquated British buses, drunk drivers and general inefficiency. Attempts to reach the wildlife reserve at Ngorongoro Crater in Northern Tanzania, either by bus or hitchhiking, had to be aborted due to the complete absence of the former and the failure of the latter. Alternative bus journeys via Iringa and Dar es Salaam brought me to Mombasa in time to be told that the ship's departure date had been brought forward by three days to 12th January. I said a little prayer of thanks that the Ngorongoro trip had failed, otherwise I would probably have missed the boat. Another plan, to visit the wonderfully attractive and peaceful, tiny resort of Lamu on the north Kenyan coast (these days no longer peaceful, courtesy of the Somalia-based terrorist group Al-Shabab) also had to be aborted and I had to make do with a quick side trip to the seaside town of Malindi.

Prior to affordable airline travel, most East African Asians wanting to visit friends and family in their original homeland had to cross the Indian Ocean by sea in such vessels as the S.S. *Kampala*. By modern cruise ship standards this was something from the Dark Ages, but it was a functional way of crossing a large expanse of water in 1971. Previously, I had made enquiries about travelling in the cheapest class, the equivalent of steerage, but was told that this was not available for '*musungus*' (white people). Later on, when I descended into the bowels of the ship, I understood why. The first sensation to hit me was the obnoxious smell, a mixture of curry, body odour and worse, then out of the murk emerged a scene of hundreds of people, babies, bunk beds, hammocks, laundry and general overcrowding.

By comparison, I was travelling in some style, in the equivalent of third class, sharing a four-berth cabin with three others for the first few days until we reached the Seychelles, where they disembarked, after which I had the cabin to myself. The only disadvantage of my situation was that the friends I had made, mostly among the European and American passengers, were in first class and although they repeatedly invited me to join them for drinks in their bar I was regularly ejected by class-conscious staff. Apart from eating and drinking, the other ways of passing the time were sunbathing – where my boredom threshold is about ten minutes – reading, watching Indian (later known as Bollywood) films (similar boredom threshold), and playing organised ship's games, where I had some considerable success at bingo.

One thousand miles due east of Mombasa, with great excitement after so long with nothing but water to look at, we had our first sighting of land. It was the Seychelles archipelago, comprising 85 islands, the largest of which is Mahe with the capital town and port, unimaginatively named Victoria. It was a very special time to be visiting because the first international airport was under construction and nearing completion, thus changing forever the character of islands that had previously only been accessible by sea.

The big decision for me was whether to disembark at Victoria and wait about ten days for the next ship to arrive or to have a whirlwind, four-hour tour around Mahe before rejoining the S.S. *Kampala*. Much as I would have liked to take the 10-day option, financial considerations dictated otherwise, but it's amazing how much can be compressed into four hours. Such tours were obviously a regular feature of island life and they were highly organised at giving the ships' visitors what they wanted. We were transported in an open-sided van, resembling an old charabanc, from Victoria into the interior, where massive granite mountains rise to 3,000 feet. It was truly a remote (for the time being) tropical island paradise. After a rapid whizz round and a quick impression of a charming mix of people speaking English and French-based creole, we returned to the port to embark on the remaining 1,750-mile voyage to our destination.

Prior to the ship's arrival in Bombay (not yet known as Mumbai), my lifetime travel experience had been limited to Africa (south of the Equator) and a few countries in Western Europe. I was familiar with big cities, after all I was a Londoner and had visited Nairobi, Johannesburg and others in Africa, but nothing had prepared me for the onslaught to my senses of arrival in

Bombay. Despite familiar architecture such as Victoria Terminus, the Gateway of India and the Taj Mahal Palace Hotel (later, in 2008, the scene of a terrorist outrage), the culture shock was massively greater than I'd experienced on my arrival in Zambia 18 months previously.

Even as we drew alongside the quay there seemed to be a multitude of people milling about and the sensation of entering a human anthill was intensified as I made my way into the city. The sheer mass of humanity was overwhelming, some very rich, some middle class but the vast majority very poor. Even in Africa I had never seen poverty like this with whole families living on the streets, each jealously guarding their tiny few feet of space and the lucky ones having taken residence in new sewer pipes lying at the side of the road prior to being buried underground, a flimsy curtain at each end offering a modicum of privacy.

Through one of the Indian teachers at my school in Zambia I had an introduction to a well-to-do Indian family and was treated to a tour of the city including the well-known sights, also the affluent suburbs and, at the other end of the spectrum, the 'street of cages' where vast numbers of prostitutes, many little more than children, in multi-storey buildings make their seedy offers, which left me wondering at the human misery behind this grotesque façade. The tourist itinerary also included a one-hour harbour cruise to the fascinating Elephanta Caves to visit the enormous 8th century rock-cut shrine on the hillside of the island, offering the uninitiated, such as me, a glimpse into the world of Hindu gods and goddesses.

Part of the attraction of travelling to India was the anticipation of eating Indian food, but it soon became evident that the meals on offer were nothing like my favourite curries at Indian restaurants in the UK. In the first place, it was mostly vegetarian and even the plates were different, especially in the cheap restaurants where I could afford to eat, the food being served on metal trays with segments to separate the different items. Try as I might I could not become adept at eating with my hands. Using a chapati to scoop up rice or lentils did not come easily and I would usually resort to asking, sheepishly, for a fork or spoon. It was also customary, in my mind, that an Indian meal should be accompanied by drinking lager, but this, of course, was not available, bearing in mind that prohibition existed in many Indian states. However, I did become the proud owner of a liquor permit for foreign tourists, which entitled me to consume six units per month, assuming that I could find alcohol in the sorts of places I could afford to frequent, in other words, not Western-style hotels.

At this time I was travelling with Jerry, an American I had met on the ship. It was convenient to travel together because we had both been invited to stay in New Delhi with an American couple, also from the ship, who were diplomats at the American Embassy. For some reason best known to himself Jerry thought that an appropriate gift for our hosts would be a parrot and that it would be a good idea to buy this parrot in Bombay. This explains how we came to be travelling on a very slow and smoky steam train with a parrot in a brown paper bag. How it survived the journey I will never know, but it was presented on our arrival to our hosts who said 'thank you, we'll put it with the others'.

The great shock in Delhi was the cold. In my innocence, I thought most parts of India away from the mountains were warm all year round. How wrong can you be? It was freezing and I only had light clothes suitable for Zambia and sandals. One of the disadvantages of having UK size 13 feet is that it is difficult to purchase shoes in most places and absolutely impossible in India, where some people go barefoot and the average shoe size for those who can afford them is probably about 7. The only solution was to get shoes made to measure, which turned out to be much less expensive than I feared even though the shoemaker on measuring my feet explained that they were the biggest pair of shoes he had ever made and he would have to charge extra. I wore those shoes, day in day out, until I arrived home in London.

Our stay in Delhi provided some wonderful sights and diversions, not least the Red Fort and other Mughal masterpieces. There was a stark and fascinating contrast between Old Delhi, with its teeming hordes, and the spacious splendour of the public buildings of New Delhi inspired by two famous British architects, Sir Edwin Lutyens and Sir Herbert Baker. Luckily, we had the opportunity to witness the annual Republic Day Parade, along the Rajpath and past India Gate, which is the only time I have ever seen bagpipe-playing soldiers and military trained elephants in the same celebration.

Of course, we also made a trip to Agra to visit the Taj Mahal. We set off early in a taxi on the 130-mile journey in order to be sure to return before nightfall, due to many warnings about 'dacoits' on the road after dark. In those days, in a misguided effort to protect the local automobile industry, there were basically only two models of car on Indian roads, the Premier Padmini, a Fiat copy, and the Ambassador, a copy of the Morris Oxford, made by Hindustan Motors. We travelled in the relative luxury of an Ambassador and hired a local guide on arrival in Agra who gave us an excellent and well-informed tour, including imparting the knowledge, that I had not previously known, that

Shah Jahan not only built the white marble Taj as the resting place for his beloved wife, Mumtaz Mahal, but also planned an identical black marble mausoleum for himself on the opposite bank of the Yamuna river that was never completed. The Taj Mahal did not disappoint and familiarity with the image only reinforced the wonder of seeing it in real life.

Prior to our departure, it was obvious that our guide was itching to ask us something. Jerry and I had made the trip with a Danish girl we had met in Delhi who had asked to join us and our guide enquired a few times if she was the wife or girlfriend of one of us. We had replied that she was just a travelling companion, but this clearly bothered our guide because such behaviour was outside Indian norms. He waited until she was out of earshot and plucked up the courage to ask us if we were both going to have 'carnal relations' with her that night. Our negative answer appeared to disappoint him greatly.

Jerry was given to making impetuous decisions, and he announced one evening that he was going to make a lightning quick, two-day visit to Katmandu and suggested that I should accompany him. Apparently, the flight was surprisingly cheap and I found myself before dawn the next morning setting off for the airport. I dozed on the plane and woke up, in the seat next to the window, to one of the most fabulous sights I have ever seen, a great expanse of mountains as far as the eye could see in either direction, the Himalayas in all their glory, Dhaulagiri, Annapurna, Manaslu and more, all in excess of 8,000 metres.

Jerry's next bright idea, given that we had so little time, was that we should hire motorbikes. In retrospect, I shudder with embarrassment because this was typical unthinking foreign tourist behaviour, because we roared around the Kathmandu

Valley visiting all the wonderful pagodas, temples and other sights, but we frightened countless children, old people, sacred cows and goodness knows what else on the way. Yet it was the most thrilling experience. In later years, I would visit Nepal on many occasions on work projects and often whispered a private apology for loutish behaviour while trying to stifle the memory of how enjoyable it was.

On returning from Katmandu I stayed at the YWCA (yes YWCA) in Delhi and made contact with the people from PBK tours, who confirmed that the bus to London would be leaving more or less as timetabled but that I must have a permit for entry into Pakistan. Deciding to arrange that right away, I folded my frame into the back of a three-wheeler taxi, also known as a tuk-tuk or auto rickshaw. These vehicles have probably contributed more to global warming than any others, given their vast amount of exhaust fumes, not to mention dreadful noise, but they were cheap.

After a while, the driver, now seeming very agitated, motioned to me to alight, grabbed the fare out of my hands and fled in a cloud of smoke. Looking around I realised why. Certainly he had dropped me near to the Pakistan High Commission, but he had omitted to point out that a demonstration, nay riot, was about to start and I was literally right in the middle of banner-waving demonstrators on one side and lines of police with their *lathis* raised on the other.

It turned out that an Indian plane had been hijacked to Pakistan as part of the never-ending dispute over Kashmir (still going strong today), and that a large number of Indian students had decided to make their protest at the Pakistan High Commission. I had nowhere to run, as either direction spelt disaster. Before I could decide, I heard teargas shells hitting the tarmac right next to me a moment before all hell broke loose inside my body as the gas reached my lungs, eyes and pretty much everywhere else. Running in the direction of the police seemed a bad idea, as I would have been greeted by blows from their *lathis*, so I took the preferred option of charging towards the advancing students, many of whom had wet towels over their faces. I somehow extricated myself from the melee and found a back street to lick my wounds. The really annoying thing was that I had to come back the next day to get my permit, but by then everything had returned to normal and the previous day was recorded as just another tiff in the ongoing Indo-Pakistan conflict.

The PBK bus left Delhi more or less on time. The best thing about it was that it was not as bad as some other modes of transport being used on the so-called 'hippy trail', which included passengers sitting in the backs of windowless trucks on bare wooden benches in great discomfort and unable to see the wonders of the lands they were passing through. There were also stories about a London double-decker plying the route which was, reportedly, stuck under a bridge somewhere. At least we were in a single decker coach, with proper seats and windows. Having said that, the less good news was that the bus was old, dilapidated and probably unsafe, with only one driver and only one tape, by Creedence Clearwater Revival, which was played over and over and over again. Strangely, I still listen to the music of CCR to this day.

My fellow passengers turned out to be pretty much the group you would have expected in those days, with lots of Europeans, Americans, Australians, New Zealanders and a few Indians and others from the subcontinent. Most were students but a few, like me, had been working abroad, although I was the only one who had travelled from Africa. Long hair was *de rigueur* for both sexes and my Afghan coat was one of many.

Our route was fantastic and included Amritsar, Lahore, Islamabad, Peshawar, the Khyber Pass, Jalalabad, Kabul, Kandahar, Herat, Mashhad, the southern shore of the Caspian Sea and Tehran. Thank goodness, with only one driver, we had to stop quite often and had opportunities to visit some of the famous sights along the way, such as the famous Great Mosque of Herat. The bus huffed and puffed up the steep inclines, particularly the magnificent Kabul River Gorge, but somehow kept going. Derek, our driver, got very agitated as we approached each border post and lectured us about drugs and how he would be the first one to go to prison if even the merest morsel of cannabis was found on the bus. Each border crossing took many hours and at the Afghanistan/Iran frontier post we were lined up in the freezing cold with our unpacked luggage while guards and enormous dogs searched every nook and cranny.

In nearly all places along the route we were objects of friendly curiosity by most local people, but sometimes friendly curiosity transformed into jostling and rude staring, particularly at the females, and most particularly at the blonde girls. The upside of this for the young men in the group was that we were called upon gallantly to protect and accompany the ladies; a duty that we quietly relished.

All the members of our party were welcome customers in the tea shops, cheap hotels, carpet and souvenir shops along the way and particularly welcomed by the money changers. At nearly every stop we would be approached, surreptitiously, by men whispering 'change money, very good rates'. It was usual for governments and their central banks at this time to impose unrealistic official rates of exchange which encouraged black market operations. The unofficial rates on offer from the money changers for cash dollars were much higher than those offered by the banks. Similarly, the Westerners were mostly travelling on very tight budgets and were very receptive to good offers for our hard currency. There were two guiding principles, however. Firstly, given that most money changing was done in shops in the back lanes of bazaars, you should never go alone, just to be on the safe side. Secondly, always check the money, which usually came in thick wads of low denomination notes, before leaving the premises because stories abounded of fellow travellers who had been duped by receiving wads with genuine notes on the top and bottom but plain paper in between.

We were unavoidably oblivious to the fact that we were passing through a region that would provide some of the world's major flashpoints in the coming years through wars and revolution. Little did I know in 1971 that I would be returning to Afghanistan on a work visit in 1977, the subject of another chapter, shortly before the Russian invasion in 1979. Regrettably, I have not yet had an opportunity to revisit Iran and see the wonderful sights, such as Isfahan, that there was no opportunity to visit on this trip. The Iran of today is a very different country from the one we passed through in 1971, not least in terms of female attire with many in those days not covering their heads as is required currently. Somewhere there must be a vast cemetery for statues of the Shah, or Mohammad Reza Shah Pahlavi to give him his full title, because every town and village we passed through had numerous life-size or larger figures at regular intervals, no doubt removed with great haste at the time of his exile to Egypt in

1979, followed by Ayatollah Khomeini's return from exile and appointment as Supreme Leader.

It was in Iran that the bus finally gave up the ghost. It was a minor miracle that it had got this far but in the town of Zanjan, roughly halfway between Teheran and the Turkish border, it breathed its last. We were stuck for many hours while Derek tried to find local mechanics capable of working new miracles, but all to no avail.

It was at this point that the owner of P Beesley (Kingston) Ltd arrived driving a bus heading towards Delhi. He must have cursed his bad luck at the timing of his arrival; a day earlier he could have passed by untroubled, but now he faced a busload of agitated customers all wanting compensation to cover our onward travel costs. After a long negotiation and covert threats to impound his other bus unless he paid up, he did so, not enough to get us to London but at least enough to help us on our way.

We were now on our own, and most opted to travel together as far as Istanbul on public transport. To our surprise, Iranian and Turkish long-distance buses provided an efficient service and were greatly superior to our old PBK coach. Having been removed from our Western travel bubble we now had to behave in a manner more appropriate to local surroundings, including sometimes stifling criticism or comments. On one occasion, I watched as a young mother failed in her efforts to quieten a persistently crying baby, resulting in her husband grabbing his wife's head and banging it roughly against the bus window, presumably to teach her a lesson. My mild gesture of reproach was met with a threatening stare that clearly told me to mind my own business.

It was a great relief to arrive in Istanbul and stop travelling for a few days. At last the weather was warmer after unremitting cold all the way from Delhi and I was beginning to recover from the illness, probably dysentery, that had laid me low since Iran. Such experiences have to be accepted as par for the course when travelling in this way, but the luxury of a Turkish bath, followed by sleeping in a comfortable bed in a cheap but clean hotel, was indescribably wonderful. I had no time pressures now, so I elected to stay several days in this one place after so long with incessant travel. Istanbul is a captivating city, both the European and Asian sides, which were still only linked by ferries at this point as the first bridge across the Bosphorus was in the early stages of construction and would not be opened until 1973. Apart from the ferries there were very enjoyable boat trips up to the Black Sea and around the Sea of Marmara. Topkapi Palace, home of the sultans and their harems, the world-famous Blue Mosque and many other attractions, provided wonderful opportunities to be a tourist at leisure. My recovered stomach was also enjoying visits to the numerous pudding shops to consume the famous baklava and halva, not to mention the more prosaic, but equally delicious, custard and rice pudding.

Now that I was back on the edge of Europe, I thought it would be a terrible shame not to make a side trip to Athens and Crete, and calculated that I could afford bus journeys to Thessaloniki and onwards to Athens, then by boat from the port of Piraeus via some Aegean Islands to Crete and back, but I would then need to hitchhike from Athens to Corfu, take the ferry to Brindisi, and then hitchhike all the way back to London. That was the plan, simple really, and it almost worked out like that except with modifications along the way. At one point in Greece, having visited the Parthenon and other wonderful sights, I was not having much luck hitchhiking along the north coast of the Peloponnese until I was approached by a policeman. I thought I might be arrested for some misdemeanour, but he pointed to my map and indicated that he wanted to know my intended destination. I pointed to Corfu (Kerkyra) and he then stopped every vehicle that came along the road until he found a suitable lorry, then indicated for me to get in. Thanks to my kindly Good Samaritan, I arrived just before dark.

While on the Corfu to Brindisi ferry I met three young Americans, two guys and a girl, travelling around Europe in an old VW campervan, who kindly offered me a lift to Rome in their already overcrowded vehicle. In fact, the overloading became even more apparent when we all tried to sleep that night in the vehicle in a service area on the way to the Bay of Naples. It was one of those nights when you reconcile yourself to getting no sleep at all but try not to move in order to avoid disturbing others. Further disappointment ensued when we arrived at Pompeii to be told that there was a national museum keepers' strike, scheduled to last for some days. Our attempt to climb over a wall, at least to get a look at the ruins, was met with threats of calling the police. It would be another 35 years before I succeeded in returning to this part of Italy and seeing Pompeii properly.

The museum keepers, and their refusal to work, also put the kibosh on my attempts to visit most of the Roman remains in Rome. By this stage I was past caring too much and just wanted to get home. After a frustratingly slow hitchhike from Rome to Paris – I always found hitchhiking in France the worst in Europe – I spent all my remaining money on a train ticket from Paris to London. Long before the Channel Tunnel and Eurostar, the trains on this route linked with the Calais/Dover ferry, and I remember feeling strangely emotional as the white cliffs came into view.

Nearly 50 years later the experiences of this trip are still more vivid in my mind than many other travels in later years. It was raw, uncomfortable and probably the most intrepid thing I have ever done, providing a warm feeling of achievement after it was all over. The thought that this experience might have been replaced by a quick flight home from Lusaka does not bear thinking about.

CHAPTER 4

INDUSTRIAL ESPIONAGE, 1974-1977

'I'm not giving any information to the Communist Intelligence Unit' said the irate person at the other end of the telephone line in response to my request for information about production levels in the textile industry. I heard myself saying, not for the first time, 'No sir, not the Communist Intelligence Unit but the Economist Intelligence Unit, we are part of the same group as the Economist newspaper and a highly respected business information and publishing company'.

A ripple of laughter went round the ballroom at Spencer House in St James's Place in London as my colleagues realised that this fairly common mistake had been repeated. Quite why the founders of the company had chosen a name that suggested an espionage link I don't know, but I wasn't going to question it, I was just glad to be there. In fact, I couldn't believe my luck to have been offered a job at the EIU after a period of several ups and downs.

Our working surroundings were amazing, especially to someone who had just come from a windowless office in Pall Mall with only a tiny skylight that the occasional pigeon dropped through. In stark contrast, Spencer House had been the town house of the Spencer family, with a grand staircase, rooms with decorated ceilings, a ballroom with chandeliers, which was my office shared with ten others, and Grecian urns galore. It is widely recognised as London's most magnificent 18th-century mansion. More than 40 years later, in 2019, I paid £15 to have an official tour of the house, magnificently restored by Lord Rothschild and now partially open to the public.

The working conditions were as genteel as the surroundings. The start of the working day was 10am and some colleagues who found that too onerous drifted in later. Long lunches were fairly standard, especially if entertaining clients; this was the 1970s after all. The younger consultants often played croquet at lunchtime in the garden adjoining Green Park with views across to Buckingham Palace. Having said all that, you were expected to produce results, and if your work wasn't up to scratch you didn't last long.

Life was good at this time. Recently married, we had just enough money to get our feet on the first rungs of the property ladder and, for the first time in my life, enough to enjoy a few luxuries like foreign holidays. Work promotion followed and we started to enjoy a better standard of living, in spite of the fact that this was the era of the 1973/4 oil crisis, the three-day week, industrial strife and the intense bombing campaign of the Provisional IRA in London, some of the blasts being only a short distance from our office in St James's.

I worked in the EIU's Industrial Market Research Division. Market research sounded rather like asking housewives about what they bought in Tesco. Nothing wrong with that, but our work was business-to-business research for large international clients, researching new market opportunities, so I sometimes embroidered the truth a bit when telling friends about my job by describing it as industrial espionage

In fact, this was not so far from the truth. Most clients wanted to find out secrets about their competitors or customers. Often we invented elaborate cover stories to camouflage our real purpose, saying that we were researching an article for one of the many publications of the group, which was true, but the main purpose of the undercover activity was the report for the fee-paying client. Some jobs were so secret that even other staff members were supposed to be kept in the dark. For many years a small team worked on 'the diamond job', which we all knew about, but woe betide anyone who spoke about it outside the office.

Long before the internet was invented, when business information systems were in their infancy, our prime working method was to telephone senior managers, often at managing director or marketing director level, to seek face-to-face meetings. Such methods would be hopeless today, but it's surprising how often mention of the Economist opened doors.

Typically, each project lasted a few weeks and we had to become instant experts in whatever subject matter landed on our desks. I researched the markets for construction equipment, Italian wine, clothing, baby foods, agricultural vehicles, animal feed, car components, among others in a variety of countries in Europe.

On the basis of attending a couple of terms of night school in German, I had ill-advisedly written on my EIU application form that I spoke the language moderately well. This exaggeration was soon exposed when my new boss, Harold, turned out to be German born. He called me into his office one day and explained, in German, that he needed another consultant to undertake projects in West Germany. I understood the gist of what he was saying but the perplexed look on my face gave away my limitations. Never mind said Harold, he would send me to the Goethe Institute in Exhibition Road, South Kensington, every morning for six weeks for intensive instruction.

Thus I embarked on numerous projects covering the length and breadth of the country. My heart sank one day when I was told that my next job was to report on the German market for fishhooks. It would be difficult to find anyone with less knowledge or less interest in the subject. I had been fishing once in my life and found it the most boring experience; why sit still beside a river or canal when you could be going for an enjoyable walk instead? Yet fishhooks turned out to be my passport to the best of times during this period. The client was so pleased with the report that they commissioned a study of the USA market and I was to do the fieldwork with a colleague.

This was exciting news, my first trip to the Americas. We landed in New York on 19th March 1976 and over the next five weeks I visited nine US states and two Canadian provinces, not a bad introduction to North America. New York's reputation for foreign visitors could not have been lower at this time; crime-ridden, a subway system that looked like a war zone with armed police in many carriages and taxi drivers who appeared to compete with each other to be the rudest in the city. I expected to hate it but absolutely loved the energy, excitement, views, famous buildings and sights.

The client gave us a list of contacts to be visited and I expected competition from my colleague to be allocated Florida and the southern states but, surprisingly, he was happy to go off to Chicago and Detroit while I booked my flight to Miami. I hired the biggest car I could afford on my expenses allowance, twice the length of my car in England, and set off to places such as Miami Beach and the Florida Keys, asking bewildered fishing tackle wholesalers and retailers a load of questions about fishhooks. These guys were not accustomed to having a 'limey' visit their premises with seemingly bizarre questions, but never mind, I was having great fun cruising around in my crazy vehicle and stopping at diners to eat mega portions of steak and french fries, although that novelty wore off quite quickly.

Next stop was Memphis Tennessee, which was rather disappointing with not much to see other than peering through the gates of Graceland. I didn't know that the following year it would become a shrine to Elvis. The next road trip took in Hot Springs Arkansas, Shreveport Louisiana and Gainesville Texas and concluded in Dallas, not yet famous for the soap opera of the same name, but infamous as the location of the JFK assassination 13 years before. A visit to the Book Depository at Dealey Plaza revealed very little to commemorate that unforgettable day.

After a few more trips, the work visit was concluded and I flew to Regina, Saskatchewan to join my wife, who had arranged to stay with an old friend from England who now lived in Canada. This was a totally different experience. Regina, previously known in the 19th century by the translated Cree name 'Pile of Bones', was just emerging from the deep winter snows that isolate it by overland routes for months on end. To celebrate this release our hosts drove us to Saskatoon, a journey of 160 miles each way, through probably the most boring scenery I have ever seen consisting of flat prairie and wheat lands, with nothing to break the monotony except occasional grain elevators.

Our next stop could not have been more different – Niagara Falls on both the Canadian and US sides. Conveniently, I had a relative, appropriately named Uncle Sam, who lived with his wife in the US town of Niagara Falls and we enjoyed wonderful American hospitality. Out of politeness, I did not mention that I found the Falls a bit tacky in comparison to the more unspoiled Victoria Falls, particularly when the former were illuminated by multi-coloured floodlights.

Our trip ended in Boston after another road trip through upstate New York, Rhode Island and Massachusetts, all very interesting and enjoyable except that this was the period of the 1976 anti-busing, race riots and we had to carefully plot a route in and around Boston that avoided the troublesome locations, identifiable from local newspapers, for fear that we might be in danger if we inadvertently strayed into the affected parts of town. We flew home on Pan-Am, still one of the most glamorous airlines in this period, before decline set in, exacerbated by disasters such as the Lockerbie terrorist bombing in 1988 and culminating in bankruptcy in 1991.

My working life at the EIU continued happily enough for nearly another year, but by early 1977 I was getting itchy feet. Work visits in Western Europe and North America were all very well, but I needed something more challenging. The wanderlust was kicking in again. Maybe it came from watching David Attenborough on television. Certainly it had something to do with a strong sense of social conscience and wanting to work, in some small way, in connection with development in poor countries. A job advert in *The Guardian* for a marketing economist to work for the wonderfully named Tropical Products Institute, a part of the Ministry of Overseas Development, provided the key to unlock this ambition.

I remember sitting in a pub around the corner from the EIU in February 1977, trying to explain to some bemused colleagues that I wanted to swap that life for one that involved travel to some of the most deprived parts of the planet. Not only that; it would also mean leaving the private sector to join the Civil Service, plus immersing myself in the strange world of agriculture, which was largely unknown to me, and downgrading from elegant Spencer House in fashionable St James's to a nondescript government building in unfashionable Clerkenwell Road. They thought I was mad, and maybe they were right.

I became an international 'expert' in March 1977 simply by starting employment with an organisation that worked on aid projects in developing countries. For the first few weeks I did not even realise that I was now an 'expert'. The transformation from London office worker to international 'expert' bestriding the world stage (well, travelling a lot anyway) was sudden and daunting. At that time, it seemed that all you needed to achieve this was to have a university degree, to be employed by an entity involved in overseas development and to be a national of one of the major aid-giving countries such as the USA or UK. That was enough to qualify you to travel the world bestowing wisdom and advice on those who lived in countries that were poorer than your own.

Within six weeks of starting my new job I was in Afghanistan working on a feasibility study, and I spent most of the next 25 years working on short-term assignments in more than 50 countries.

It took some time to become accustomed to arriving in a capital city such as Kathmandu or Damascus and then, together with other team members, being ushered into the presence of a minister or senior official with the words 'the experts have arrived'. Even more intimidating was the realisation that I was now being referred to as an expert in agriculture. Having grown up in a council flat over some shops in a London suburb, with not much more than a window box to cultivate, I was not well placed to be an agricultural adviser. Of course, my superiors knew I had no agricultural expertise; they had employed me for my knowledge of marketing and economics, about which I could at least pass muster fairly convincingly, but I was now working for an agricultural institute and the expectation in the aid-receiving countries was that I should know something about agriculture. I was, after all, an 'expert'.

As a highly, even painfully, conscientious person, I now attempted to acquire some knowledge about cocoa, coconuts, cassava and hundreds of other agricultural products. I read books, enrolled in courses and generally became a thoroughgoing bore about commodities, the Common Agricultural Policy and every other agri-related subject. I envied those of my colleagues who had grown up on farms, learnt to drive a tractor before they could walk and delivered new-born lambs in the snow before school. These people also usually had a degree in agriculture or agricultural economics, subjects which were rather more directly relevant than my own BA Hons in Politics.

So, I started off my career as an international 'expert' in fear of being found out and exposed as a sham, but I gradually began to realise that all involved in the 'aid industry' were faking it to a greater or lesser extent and that I was no worse than most of the rest of them. At least my new job enabled me to indulge my passion for travel.

CHAPTER 5

AFGHANISTAN, 1977

My first experience as an international 'expert' is best forgotten. It was a meeting at the Ministry of Agriculture in Kabul in April 1977. It was an inauspicious start.

I had flown into Kabul with Eddie, a Dutch agronomist, by an extremely convoluted route involving stops in Paris, Istanbul and Tehran. Eddie was an old hand with lots of experience of Afghanistan, which explained why he was a member of a British team funded by British aid. Foreigners on British aid teams were not a common feature at that time, unlike today when it is *de rigueur* to have a nationality and a racial mix and, of course, a gender balance. I had met Eddie once before, at a team meeting held at the Ministry of Overseas Development (known as ODM to distinguish it from the Ministry of Defence MOD, an organisation you would not want to get confused with on missions to some of the more sensitive parts of the world). The main thing I had noticed about Eddie at that first meeting was that he was an incessant nose-picker. Not the sort of person who has a sly dig when he thinks that no one is looking but a 'couldn't care less', remorseless, inveterate nose-picker. If they had nose-picking as an Olympic event, the Netherlands would get one of their rare gold medals.

On arrival at Kabul airport, tired and bedraggled, we were met by one of the British Embassy's local staff with a note from our team leader, Peter Street, saying that on our way to the embassy compound where the team was based, we were to go via the Ministry of Agriculture to pay a courtesy call on the Acting Deputy Minister of Agriculture. This news was met with a number of Dutch profanities by Eddie, but I was keen as mustard and eager to make a start on saving the world, beginning with Afghanistan. We made our way through the claustrophobic chaos of the airport, into the exciting chaos of the streets of the city and eventually drew up at a drab official building with an ominous mural of the British garrison in Kabul being defeated in 1841. This was the Ministry of Agriculture.

We arrived during a power cut and had to use the stairs rather than the lift – more Dutch oaths. Over the years, after some unpleasant experiences, I have learned never to trust the lifts in public buildings in developing countries, and this was the first of many thousands of flights of stairs to be climbed on official business. We were led down several darkened corridors with hundreds of people milling about or sitting aimlessly in offices. The one common feature of all the people who were on view in the building was that no one was doing anything that remotely resembled work. In my innocence I imagined that this situation came about because of the power cut, but when I visited the ministry again on a bright, clear day with the electricity supply working normally, the situation was exactly the same – no one was working. This was another part of the learning curve of the novice international expert – in most developing countries, with few exceptions, the only civil servants who do any work are some of the more senior officials and some of the staff who work directly for them. Otherwise, the vast majority of public servants get by with working at about a 20% efficiency level, and some don't even get out of single figures.

Eddie and I were shown into the Acting Deputy Minister's waiting room and a male secretary motioned us to sit down. The minutes ticked by, accompanied by Dutch oaths, and slowly an hour passed. Eddie explained the drill: a minister will always keep you waiting, unless you are of equivalent rank, which we were certainly not. A deputy minister will keep you waiting longer because he aspires to be a minister. An acting deputy minister is pretty low down the pecking order and will keep you waiting the longest of all because it inflates his self-importance and sends a signal to underlings in the ministry: 'Look, I'm important enough to keep these foreign experts waiting'.

Eventually we were shown into the office of the Acting Deputy Minister, which contained a bustling crowd of people who came in and went out at intervals. The ADM made appropriate apologies for keeping us waiting and welcomed us to Afghanistan. Through an interpreter he asked if it was our first visit. Eddie spoke for a while about the previous projects he had been associated with and the ADM looked suitably impressed. My only previous visit had been passing through the country on a 'hippy bus' in 1971, which I decided against mentioning, thinking that it might seem rather less relevant and impressive than Eddie's Afghan CV.

As the meeting proceeded, I became aware that Eddie's nasal hobby had reached heroic proportions. I had formed the habit when in his company of sitting with my hand at the side of my head with my elbow resting on my knee. In this way I could screen my view from the unpleasant spectacle. But round the side of my hand I became aware that Eddie was not only digging deeper than usual but was also giving close scrutiny to the outcome on each occasion. Covered in collective team embarrassment for this behaviour I looked over to the ADM to see if he had noticed. He had also adopted a posture with his hand at the side of his head and I wondered if he was using the same screening technique as myself.

The secretary entered the room with a leather-bound folder containing letters and other documents for the ADM to sign. I wish I had a penny for every minute spent waiting during my career while the signing ritual proceeded. Most meetings are interrupted in this way because ministers and senior officials are the only people who can sanction any activity. In one African country the chitty to allow me to buy petrol for my team's trip up-country had to be signed by the minister himself.

While the papers were being signed, I took the opportunity to peep round my hand to check if things had subsided. To my enormous relief I saw that both Eddie's hands were resting in his lap, suggesting that there was at least a pause in excavations. But then, horror of horrors, the reason for the pause became clear; Eddie was asleep.

I tried to gather my thoughts. He was too far away to kick and it would be too obvious to get up, cross the room and give him a shake. I felt vulnerable. Suppose the ADM started asking me complicated questions about the project. We were there to do a feasibility study on the storage and marketing of wheat, Afghanistan's staple food, and devise a price stabilisation scheme. Quite a complicated subject especially when I had no idea what had transpired with the members of the team who were already in Kabul. They had been in the country for a couple of weeks but telephone communication with London at that time was well-nigh impossible and the only news we had received was a couple of short telex messages along the lines of, 'Don't forget to bring the gin with you'.

When the ADM returned his attention to me, I started babbling about some aspect of wheat storage in Afghanistan that I had read about in the briefing papers. This was a mistake. The interpreter looked quizzical and the ADM appeared absolutely mystified. I realised later that ministers have little or no interest in individual projects and are only going through the motions of receiving courtesy calls from visiting teams because it fits into the wider picture of maintaining relations with the aid-giving countries. After a bit more aimless chatter the meeting broke up, I gave Eddie a kick and we departed.

The scene that met our eyes when we arrived at the British embassy compound was like stepping back into a Kipling novel. The main mansion, supposedly built on the instructions of Lord Curzon, resembled a wedding cake covered in icing sugar. The ambassador's enormous black Daimler was parked outside. There were several other buildings and houses, one of which was allocated to our team for the duration of our stay. Most remarkable of all were the gardens, which consisted of irrigated and manicured lawns and flower beds cared for by teams of gardeners. The overall effect was magnificent but also ridiculous. Here we were in one of the poorest and most arid countries on the planet living in plush and lush surroundings that suggested, contrary to the evidence of history, that the Raj had made it to Kabul and was still alive and well.

Goodness knows, the British had tried hard enough to bring Afghanistan into the empire in the nineteenth century, but the fiercely independent Afghans always managed, eventually, to rebuff the advances. The competition of the British and Russian imperial powers to gain influence in central Asia, as described by Peter Hopkirk in *The Great Game*, went on over many decades, costing many lives in the process. History, as they say, has a tendency to repeat itself. Here I was, in 1977, metaphorically waving the Union Jack as a member of an official British aid mission to Afghanistan and before long, although we had no idea at the time, the mighty Russian bear would reappear over the horizon.

The imperial connections extended to the food we were served. An Afghan cook employed by the embassy was assigned to our house for the duration of our stay. I met many such gentlemen (cooks were usually men at this time) in later trips to other countries, particularly in east and central Africa. A typical meal might start with brown Windsor soup, followed by lamb chops, boiled potatoes and canned peas, with apple pie and custard for dessert. Any suggestion that he might serve a local dish for a change one evening would usually be met with incredulity and be quietly ignored. My abiding memory of the unique culinary contribution of this particular cook was the ice-cold stewed rhubarb served for breakfast each day. This was quite a surprise on the first morning, but after that I found myself really looking forward to it each day for the following month.

Looking back on our time in Afghanistan in 1977, it is clear that we were extremely privileged to be witnessing the last period of relative freedom and normality in a country that was soon to be plunged into more than 40 years, to date, of war and mayhem. The Russian invasion of 1979 was driven by the desire of cold-hearted leaders in Moscow to give the USSR an outlet to the Indian Ocean and, perhaps, act as a stepping-stone to capturing other prizes such as the oilfields of the Persian Gulf. But the Russian troops, mostly consisting of bewildered young conscripts, never succeeded in washing their boots in the Indian Ocean and, instead, got bogged down in an exhausting and ultimately pointless guerrilla war. The *mujahideen* eventually prevailed and the Russians made an ignominious withdrawal in 1989, but worse was to come in the form of Afghan warring factions, followed by the vicious rule of the Taliban, which provided a home for Osama bin Laden's al-Qaeda training camps, and then the US-led invasion of 2001.

The effect on the ordinary people of Afghanistan, who survived this prolonged trauma, can only be imagined. I got an impression of what life was like for some displaced Afghans when I saw conditions in the refugee camps in the border area of Pakistan in the 1980s. Some people lived in these dreadful conditions for years and years, but they were the lucky ones compared to many of those who suffered inside Afghanistan.

Little did we realise in 1977 that our journeys throughout Afghanistan in pursuit of information about wheat production, storage and marketing would provide us with images of the end of an era. It is not that the situation in 1977 was particularly idyllic, it was not, but that what was to follow was so much worse. Afghanistan in 1977 was one of the poorest countries on the planet with a very low level of per capita income. Because the country was landlocked without significant oil deposits or other resources, and large parts of it were mountainous or semi-desert, life was a struggle for survival for most of the population.

Many of the rural population were scratching a living from small patches of land. Those dependent upon rainfed agriculture led a very precarious existence, because if the rains failed at the required growing time, the crop failed and the family had neither food to eat nor a crop to sell. We saw many examples of fields where sheep and goats had been set loose to feed on the pathetic remnants of a failed wheat crop that would never produce a single grain to be baked into naan bread.

The more fortunate farming families had access to some form of irrigation. Over many centuries Afghans had developed various ingenious means of transporting water from the few places it existed, in a largely arid and barren environment, to the fields where it was needed to irrigate the crops. In some places amazing underground tunnels ran for miles and miles from rivers to farms that lit up the landscape with their greenness. Few of these magnificent irrigation systems survived the following years of turmoil.

The great advantage in being an international expert in agriculture, as opposed to, say, industry or banking, is that you have a wonderful excuse to travel around the rural areas. Capital cities are interesting enough, but they seldom give a flavour of the real character of a country and some seem like an alien imposition totally removed from the rest of the nation. Accordingly, I have always taken every opportunity to get out of the cities at the earliest opportunity and head for the countryside.

The only disadvantage of this approach is that it usually

means swapping city comforts for some rather strange forms of accommodation, separated by vast distances and connected by roads that appear to have been designed to provide maximum human discomfort. Over the years I have slept in tents, in cars, in rat-infested hovels and under the stars, while also travelling over roads that in some cases I would not have known were supposed to be roads unless told so by the local people. However, I should not try to give the impression that I am some kind of tough guy like my namesake Indiana. Nor am I a Wilfred Thesiger type, happy to be traipsing around the Empty Quarter of Saudi Arabia with only camels and a few Bedu for company. Nothing could be further from the truth. People like Thesiger actively seek out such hardships in order to test themselves, whereas I actively seek out air-conditioning, comfortable beds and English breakfasts wherever possible.

However, such things do have to be forsaken from time to time in order to enjoy experiences that transcend the discomforts. During my stay in Afghanistan I was fortunate to be able to make two long trips outside Kabul, but before that I had to endure two weeks of meetings in the capital following what I would soon learn was the accepted pattern for aid missions. You always start with meetings with ministers or senior officials in the Ministry of Agriculture and other relevant ministries such as planning or industry and trade. You then visit the Central Statistics Office to collect all relevant data (which you take with a very large pinch of salt). Next you do the rounds of the offices of all the international institutions such as the World Bank, IMF, the Food and Agriculture Organisation (FAO) of the United Nations, and then the local representatives of the main aid-giving countries such as the Americans and the Germans.

It was about this time that I started to recognise two failings of the 'aid industry'. Firstly, there was enormous duplication between the work of the various agencies and secondly, the agencies themselves were highly competitive. The evidence of duplication was easy to see in 1977. Already the World Bank, FAO, USAID (the United States Agency for International Development) and the German aid agency had written reports about the very subject that the British team was here to study. We managed to obtain copies of these reports, but there was no real pooling of resources as would have been sensible. In countries such as Afghanistan, there would usually be a severe shortage of viable projects suitable for aid funding and therefore each agency, both multilateral and bilateral, tended to investigate every possibility, with the inevitable consequence of duplicated effort. The agencies acted like competing commercial companies instead of all pulling in the same direction. This resulted in lots of aid missions to the target countries, and many developing countries' governments did not have the capacity to deal with all the visiting teams and their reports.

Armed with the necessary, but difficult to obtain, official permits to travel round the country, we were ready to venture forth. My first trip was to the south of Afghanistan, following the road from Kabul to Ghazni, on to Kandahar (later to be made infamous as the home of the Taliban) and beyond to a place in the middle of nowhere called Lashkargar. I had travelled this same road six years before on the 'hippy bus' to the sounds of Creedence Clearwater Revival blaring out from the speakers to the astonishment of nearby herdsmen and their goats. Now we were a very different group. I was travelling with Peter Street, together with an interpreter and a driver, both provided by the embassy. We visited grain markets and grain silos, the latter mostly built with Russian aid, and took every opportunity, within the limits of the time available, to stop and talk along the way to farmers who were growing wheat, consuming it as a subsistence crop and hoping to have a surplus for sale.

It has often struck me that so-called international experts have a great advantage over professional travel writers, such as Paul Theroux and Bill Bryson, who have to invent reasons for travelling and speaking to the local population. As a foreigner in a country such as Afghanistan it is often quite difficult to meet ordinary local people other than hotel staff and taxi drivers, but the international specialist working on an agricultural study has a built-in need to visit remote rural communities and seek out opportunities for talking to local people. Having done this in places as far apart as the Pacific islands and deepest Africa, I can say that the reaction is nearly always exactly the same – enormous hospitality, even from people living at the very margins of existence, and a cup of the local beverage. In some places this may be alcoholic, such as a bombshell drink called *rakshi* in the hills of Nepal, but in Afghanistan it is always a cup, or more usually a glass, of *chai* (tea).

The most fascinating aspect of foreign travel for me is observing the local people. It is intriguing to see how they live, what racial groups they belong to, what religions they follow, what political opinions they hold, how Westernised they are, how they make a living, what they wear, what languages they speak and how they interact with each other, particularly in terms of the treatment of children and women. On this trip we were mostly travelling among the largest tribal group in the country, the Pashtun (also known as Pathans), who constituted about 40 per cent of the population, but later I would also visit the areas predominantly populated by other groups within the mosaic of Afghan tribes such as the Tajiks, Uzbeks and Hazaras, the latter being descended from the remnants of Genghis Khan's army.

During the first trip we also saw one of the most colourful and unusual groups of people in Afghanistan at that time, the Kuchis (a word meaning 'nomad' in the Dari language). According to the Afghan Central Statistics Office (if it can be believed), in the Islamic year 1355 (corresponding to mid-March 1976 to mid-March 1977), nomads accounted for 2.4 million out of a total national population of 17.1 million. In 1977, these nomadic people were quite unlike the rest of the population. They wandered over vast areas with their camels, goats and sheep, seeking pasture for their animals in a very inhospitable and arid landscape. The women were particularly noticeable because they wore flamboyant coloured clothes and did not cover their faces. The men had a rather fearsome reputation and were known to be always armed with rifles. According to our interpreter, they pursued a hobby of shooting at the telegraph poles that crossed the barren wasteland in order to see the sparks flying which, apparently, made a rather fine firework display but did not help with building up the telecommunications network of the country. But the Kuchis were not on the phone, so what did they care?

Peter and I had discussed the need to speak to some Kuchis about their role in carrying grain from one place to another. In addition to their camels, some Kuchis had old, battered pick-up trucks and added to their meagre income by buying and selling grain. We had decided that it would not be advisable to try and speak to them when they were on the move but rather to look out for an encampment that was near the road. A suitable opportunity presented itself en route from Kandahar to Lashkagar. An encampment of four or five tents was located about 200 metres from the road. Our interpreter advised against driving all the way over to the tents on the basis that the Kuchis might think that we were government officials or tax inspectors. If we parked the car by the road and walked to the tents it would be obvious that we were not armed and, hopefully, that we were harmless. Our driver, conscious of the need to preserve the safety of the car and himself, bravely volunteered to stay with the vehicle (probably with the engine running).

The three of us set off across the barren landscape. The 200-metre walk gave us ample opportunity to take in the scene. The tents were open sided in the Arabic style and revealed the sheer lack of possessions of these people. All they had in the world seemed to amount to no more than a few carpets and some pots and pans. Their main wealth resided in their animals, and a scrawny lot they looked. Some rather mangy-looking camels were tethered close to the camp and in the distance we could see their goats seeking out scattered tufts of vegetation that would certainly not rank as pasture in most parts of the world.

A line of men had formed in front of the tents. Groups of women, with children clinging to their skirts, took up position in the background. The men looked suspicious and the wisdom of making these enquiries began to look increasingly doubtful. I weighed up the possibility of turning and running but did not fancy the possibility of dodging bullets.

On arrival at the camp we gave the usual greetings and our interpreter attempted to explain our purpose. Goodness knows what he said to them, because the concept of a group of foreigners coming from the other side of the world to ask questions about their grain trading habits must have seemed obscure in the extreme, but whatever he said worked. Their faces turned to smiles and we were invited over to one of the tents to drink *chai*.

I began to relax and was just about to accept an offer to sit down on one of the stacks of carpets positioned outside the tent when one of the biggest of the men grabbed me by the arm and yanked me backwards. My life flashed before me. The smiles had obviously been false and we were about to have our throats slit. I thought of shouting to Peter something along the lines of, 'Tell my wife I love her' when the interpreter jumped forward and explained that I had nearly sat on grandma. Apparently, it is the custom amongst the Kuchis for people who are ill to be rolled up in a carpet and laid out in the sun. This sounds more like a form of death by mummification, particularly as this part of Afghanistan experiences summer temperatures almost as hot as anywhere in the world, but who knows? Don't knock it unless you've tried it. Sometime later, when my mother-in-law was not feeling very well, I did offer to wrap her in a carpet and put her outside her house in Malvern, Worcestershire, but she quite unreasonably refused to go along with the experiment.

After many apologies for giving me a shock, we sat down on unoccupied carpets and enjoyed tea and conversation with our hosts. Even our reluctant driver was enticed over from the car. Once it became clear that we posed no threat, the Kuchis, like most people in the world, with the possible exception of the Swiss, became extremely hospitable. They would have shared their small quantity of food with us if we had not made excuses about needing to reach our destination before nightfall.

An article published in December 2003 by Refugees International entitled 'Forgotten People: the Kuchis of

Afghanistan' says that only a small number of Kuchis still follow their traditional livelihood of nomadic herding, moving from summer pastures in the highlands to winter grazing at lower elevations. The war against the Russians, followed by civil war, disrupted their lives and many became refugees in Pakistan or displaced persons within Afghanistan. More recently the Kuchis have experienced a range of problems including landmines on their routes, hostility from other tribes and difficulty in restocking herds due to lack of finance and drought-affected pastures. Many Kuchis say they want to return to a nomadic lifestyle, but they face an uphill struggle.

Having departed the Kuchi camp we continued on our way through Helmand province, an unknown corner of the world at that time but a major feature on BBC News broadcasts from 2006 when the British army were stationed there, fighting against the Taliban. Our night stop provided a complete contrast with the day's earlier experience. We spent the night in an American rest house in Lashkargar, a small place in semi-desert conditions, many miles from anywhere of any size. The American aid programme had some local projects and a dozen or so Americans were living in this place. The Americans one meets in developing countries are an odd bunch. A few of them 'go native' (bare feet, beads, that sort of thing) but the great majority seem hell-bent on trying to create little Americas wherever they find themselves with virtually no attention paid to the local surroundings or culture. In many countries they create mini-towns with high walls and armed guards to keep out the local population, except servants and suppliers, and build burger bars, cinemas to show American films and shopping malls that ship in virtually all their requirements from the USA. I would readily agree that the

British one meets in developing countries are an odd bunch too, but they are more diverse in the way they interact with local circumstances, whereas the Americans all seem to be out of the same mould. They give the impression of wanting to live in the US rather than where they are.

In the rest house, powerful generators provided air conditioning, lighting and power. After a hot shower and an excellent dinner of steak and fries we were invited to participate in their regular Wednesday night session of a game that the English would call bingo. As I sat in the air-conditioned restaurant surrounded by vending machines stuffed with Coca Cola and candy bars, with the whirring noise of the ice machine nearly blotting out the sound of Roy Orbison coming from the jukebox, it struck me that the scene was more reminiscent of Arkansas than Afghanistan. We were in a little capsule that was physically a few miles away from the Kuchi camp but was light years away in every other respect. The only common feature was the wonderful hospitality.

At this point, if I was a Wilfred Thesiger type, I would claim that I would much rather have slept in the Kuchi camp under the stars, listening to the sounds of nature rather than Roy Orbison. On a few occasions I have spent the night in a similar fashion and it has probably done my soul good and made me a more sympathetic person, but it is also bloody uncomfortable. The toilet arrangements alone are a nightmare, not to mention the need to smilingly accept food and drink that is extremely difficult to get down and which you know for sure is going to come back up again. No, it would be dishonest to pretend that I did not enjoy the ice-cold Budweiser on our arrival at the rest house and the waffles for breakfast before our departure, and everything else in between. But it would also be dishonest to pretend that the Americans can live in this way without creating a gulf between themselves and the local population which is a serious impediment to achieving the aid goals they set themselves.

My second trip was undertaken in the company of Eddie. Our plan was to visit the north of the country, crossing the massive Hindu Kush mountains, an extension of the Himalayas that diagonally bisect Afghanistan, starting in the north-east corner and extending for hundreds of miles and reaching altitudes in excess of 5,000 metres. Eddie proposed that we should not take the easy route, which was the tarmac road built by the Russians. 'Big enough to take the largest Russian tanks' said Eddie with great prescience. Indeed the road did carry Russian tanks before long; it was also the scene of hundreds of Russian and Afghan deaths in 1982 when a series of unexplained explosions took place inside the Salang Tunnel, famous for being the highest altitude long tunnel in the world.

Instead of taking the Russian-built road, our planned route followed one of the old roads to the north, passing through Bamiyan before reaching Mazar-i-Sharif, the major city of the north. Mazar is only a short distance from the Oxus River, now known as the Amu Darya, where I remember standing on the south bank, looking north and thinking with some awe and trepidation, 'That is the Soviet Union'. In those Cold War days I was unaware whether I was looking into Turkmenistan, Uzbekistan or Tajikistan, as they all seemed to be the same. It was just the USSR. At that stage it was unthinkable to me, and probably to most other people, that only 15 years later the Cold War would be over and I, and many others, would be working on aid projects in Russia and the other former Soviet republics.

Leaving Kabul, we passed through some fertile areas renowned worldwide for the production of dried fruits, particularly sultanas and apricots, which were a major source of foreign currency earnings in those days, with exports to Europe and many other parts of the world. Today, the orchards and drying rooms are virtually all destroyed. We travelled on in our Land Rover towards the high mountain passes on the kind of roads that extreme sports enthusiasts deliberately seek out for the love of danger; roads cut out of mountainsides, with a rock face on one side and a precipice on the other. There are lots of hairpin bends and rock falls, which either totally block the road or force the road users imaginatively to find alternative routes through the undergrowth.

Afghan truck drivers, like many others of the same profession in other parts of the world where road conditions are similar, play a little game whereby they seem to be trying to push smaller vehicles over the precipices. Afghan trucks, like many others in south Asia, are often works of art with all sorts of religious and other scenes painted on any spare area of bodywork and additional decorative bits of metalwork added to the structure. European or American trucks pale into insignificance by comparison. Additional truck lights, strings of fairy lights, hanging decorations and klaxon horns, may supplement the gaudy effect, but they are wolves in sheep's clothing because their real purpose is to push you over the precipice. Luckily our driver was acquainted with the game and adopted various cat and mouse tactics to avoid disaster, though not before I had chewed my nails down to the bone.

Our first overnight stop was at Bamiyan, a small town in the mountains made famous by the nearby enormous Buddha statues carved into the sandstone rock face. Many consider these statues to be one of the wonders of the world, but today they exist only in photographs, having been blown up by the Taliban in March 2001 on the basis that they offended against an interpretation of Islamic law that disallows human images. The heads of the Buddhas had already been defaced by much earlier terrorist activity, but the bodies were more or less intact. They commanded the landscape for miles around and were one of the few sights I have seen that actually took my breath away. The impact was the greater because of the knowledge that so few people outside Afghanistan had had the opportunity to see these magnificent statues. Now they will never see them because of one of the worst acts of cultural terrorism in history.

The two Buddha statues had been built in the sixth century. They stood about half a mile apart, the larger approximately 180 feet high and the smaller, still very imposing, at about 125 feet. Apparently, it took the Taliban a number of days to destroy these colossal works of art. According to reports they started off with rocket attacks, which had little effect, so they brought in large quantities of explosives to finish the job and deprive humanity of a part of its heritage.

The statues needed to be seen at close quarters and from far away. A staircase cut out of the rock, but inside the rock face, allowed access to the head of one of the Buddhas. After a strenuous climb, passing some of the caves lived in by the Buddhist sculptors and their descendants about 1,500 years ago, it was possible to stand on the head and survey the landscape, with an area of flat, cultivated land in the foreground and a long line of mountains in the distance. In 2002 a BBC television reporter ascended the same staircase and stopped at the point where I had stepped on to the head of the Buddha; he spoke to camera with just a void behind him. The giant rock alcove, itself enormously impressive, was intact, but almost every trace of the statue was gone.

In order to take photographs and to absorb the whole scene, I descended the stairs and walked some distance away until the Buddhas would fit into the camera's viewfinder. While sitting on the ground and marvelling at the scene before me I became aware of the antics of a traffic policeman just behind me. He was engaged in one of the most pointless official exercises I have ever seen and was living proof of the maxim that if you put a person in charge of a gate he will find reasons to stop people entering rather than letting them through.

The traffic policeman was in charge of a T-junction on the main road into Bamiyan. Given that this small town was in a remote location, in the middle of a range of mountains, with awful roads in every direction, it is not surprising that the amount of traffic was very limited – probably about one vehicle every five minutes. In the centre of the junction was a raised circular plinth. The land was flat in each of the three directions, so that it was obvious that a vehicle was approaching long before it reached the junction. At this point the policeman would jump into life from his prone position in the shade of a nearby tree and race across to take up his position on the plinth. With great ceremony and full of self-importance, he would then raise his arm, indicating that the vehicle must stop. He would then hold the vehicle in that position for at least a couple of minutes while making exaggerated scrutiny of the totally empty roads in every direction. With further great ceremony and with a sweep of the arm he would indicate that the vehicle could proceed and if the driver was a little bit slow in pulling away there would be a further, exasperated gesture as if to say 'Come on, I haven't got all day'. I expect he went home in the evening and told his wife that he'd had a really hard day at work.

Our interpreter gave us the news that he had found accommodation for us for the night – in a tent. I immediately had dreadful visions of sleeping in a Kuchi-style tent alongside Eddie pursuing his objectionable habit. I need not have worried. The tents in question proved to be Mongol-style yurts with full mod cons, including beds and even en suite bathrooms. They had been built for the intrepid Western tourists that some entrepreneur had expected to come flocking to this wonderful site. This might not have been such a crazy idea but for the fact that it was probably Russian soldiers who were occupying the yurts the following year.

That evening we ate lamb kebabs and naan bread in one of the very simple local restaurants in Bamiyan, surrounded by large numbers of local people, many of them with the Mongol features of the Hazaras. Aid professionals end up eating in some extraordinarily different places ranging from ludicrously priced restaurants in five-star hotels to accepting the hospitality of poor farmers living in mud huts. But some of the best times are spent in genuinely local restaurants, patronised by local people (as opposed to the richest one per cent of the population). This restaurant was crowded, smoky and smelly, but it had a wonderful atmosphere assisted by some unusual music, at least to the Western ear. The music was provided by a band of about six people and a young singer who was making an excruciating, wailing sound, much appreciated by the local customers. This image always came back to me when reading newspaper reports of the Taliban era and their ban on all forms of music. In their wisdom, they also banned shaving, kites, photographs and lots of other things. I hope the musicians kept their instruments in a safe place during those dark days and that at least some of them were able to resume their rightful role of giving wonderful entertainment to their fellow citizens.

Some days later, after completing our work in the north, Eddie and I were scheduled to fly back from Mazar-i-Sharif to Kabul. We arrived at the airport in the morning to be told that our flight was delayed because of adverse weather conditions around Kabul. Part of the glamour of being an international expert is spending hour after hour killing time in grotty airports, very often without food, drink or access to any information about the intended flight. I never tire of explaining this to friends who seem to imagine that my working life is one long luxury holiday, Furthermore, everyone in these circumstances is usually bad-tempered and it is only a matter of time before they start regaling each other with horror stories of long delays ('I remember the time I waited 24 hours at Dar-Es-Salaam airport') or near fatal air disasters ('I realised something was wrong when the stewardesses started putting on parachutes'). I have been guilty of telling such slightly embellished tales myself, but Eddie turned out to be a past master of the genre. He had stories that would persuade you never to go near an aeroplane again, particularly not a small, ancient, Russian plane of a type with a bad crash record, which was apparently what we were waiting for to carry us to Kabul.

By chance, one of the other stranded passengers was the British ambassador. He had wisely decided not to make the trip to the north in his Daimler, although there was a story that the car had originally been driven from Pakistan to Kabul, via the Khyber Pass, which must have provided an interesting sight for the border guards, not to mention the legendary ferocious Pathan tribesmen of the region. The ambassador had the wonderfully undiplomatic name of Mr Crook. We had met him a couple of times during our stay in the embassy compound. He had always been very pleasant and courteous, but also rather distant because we were relative underlings in the overall scheme of things. He had kindly invited our team for drinks in the embassy one Sunday evening a week or two before. Prior to the appointed time we were given strict instructions by an embassy lickspittle about the format the drinks session would take. 'After being seated, a waiter will take your order for a gin and tonic; as soon as the first drink is finished the waiter will refill your glass; after that the waiters will withdraw from the room and you will make your exit after finishing the second glass and certainly within one hour of entering'.

After several hours of conversation and swapping air travel horror stories, we were told to board the plane. I am not an enthusiastic flyer at the best of times. Flights on perfectly maintained modern jumbo jets operated by one of the world's leading airlines are usually OK, but my level of anxiety gradually increases in proportion to the age of the plane, the size of the plane (the larger the better), the nationality of the airline and the state of disarray or drunkenness of the pilot. The combined efforts of Eddie and the pilot contributed to making this one of life's worst flights. As we walked out to the plane, the pilot, who was quite sober, mentioned in casual conversation that Kabul was not equipped with any form of modern landing aids and even the state of the runway lights was a bit hit and miss. Furthermore, Kabul is situated within a circle of mountains that tend to hold in cloud and pollution, thus making visibility from the air very difficult, particularly when some of the lights are not working. Apparently, that day was particularly bad for visibility. This was more information and candour than I needed. I would have preferred some simple lies about the excellent state of the plane, the airport and the weather.

As we approached the plane, Eddie chipped in with his own advice, to always check the state of the tread on a plane's tyres as an indicator of airworthiness. Following this advice was unavoidable because we were standing by a completely bald tyre at that particular moment. I thanked Eddie for the benefit of his wisdom and silently vowed always to avert my eyes from the direction of a plane's tyres in future.

Needless to say the flight was awful and became one of my own horror stories for the future. In addition to bad visibility, a violent thunderstorm blew up as we were approaching Kabul and we made several landing approaches, only for each one to be aborted and the nose pulled up sharply. My mind imagined the probable scene in the cockpit with the pilot struggling to discern something that vaguely resembled a runway light before having to give up the attempt and then concentrate on dodging round a mountain that had suddenly been revealed by a bolt of lightning. The only saving grace of this situation was that Eddie was so distracted by approaching death that he forgot to pursue his hobby. This was a small mercy indeed but one that was nevertheless welcome. Eventually the pilot managed to track down the airport, we landed and Eddie resumed you know what.

Over the following months, after the team returned from Afghanistan, a great deal of hard work went into preparing a full feasibility study report for the wheat storage and price stabilisation scheme. It was an important subject to get right for the people of Afghanistan, and I was impressed by the professionalism of my new colleagues in aiming to do the best job possible. The report was accepted and widely applauded, and the World Bank entered into negotiations to assist with the implementation of the proposals. All looked promising for a while, but developments were hampered by increasing instability in the country during 1978/9, culminating in the news in late December 1979 that Russian tanks had crossed the border.

CHAPTER 6

NEPAL, 1978

When I heard cat-like noises outside my tent, I convinced myself that it was a snow leopard. Earlier in the day we had seen snow leopard traps outside two of the villages we passed through on our trek down the Kali Gandaki river valley between the mighty mountains of Annapurna and Dhaulagiri. The traps were like mini stone houses with a live goat as bait in the back 'room' and an open front door inviting the snow leopard to enter. If it did, a trap-door device would be activated and the snow leopard would be caught. According to the villagers, several of their livestock had been killed in recent weeks and they were anxious to catch the culprit. The trap seemed to be an ingenious contrivance and everyone would be happy if it did its job, except for the goat, of course, which was sacrificed for the greater good.

At that precise moment, as I lay in my tent in the middle of the night, listening to a sort of growling-purring noise, I felt an overwhelming wave of sympathy for the goat. I also recalled reading about a project to preserve the endangered snow leopard in this part of the world and privately cursed the do-gooders for their efforts. I was absolutely petrified and not thinking very clearly. I considered shouting out to Keith in the tent immediately adjacent to mine, but dismissed this idea on the unlikely premise that the snow leopard might not realise that I was inside my tent if I kept quiet. I took this wishful thinking one step further by putting my empty rucksack over my head, thinking that the snow leopard, after clawing a hole in the tent wall, would stick its head through, see a rucksack and a sleeping bag and say to itself, 'Oh, there's no one here' and disappear into the night. Much more likely it would have said, 'He'll make a tasty late-night snack'.

I stayed in that position for a long time and eventually dozed off. I must have been in more danger of death by suffocation than by being eaten by a snow leopard. Then a scream, from just a few feet away, woke me with a start. I sat bolt upright, still with my head in the rucksack, and nearly knocked myself out on the tent pole. The combination of sleep, concussion and fear created a very befuddled state.

I tentatively removed the rucksack and attempted to take stock of the situation. Clearly the snow leopard was having Keith for breakfast. What would I tell his wife back in Bromley? Before I could compose some appropriate words, I heard a long line of muffled English swear words coming from slightly further away than the earlier scream.

'Keith, are you all right?' It transpired that he had needed a pee in the night, had come out of his tent and, forgetting that we were camped on a steeply terraced hillside, had plunged five feet over the edge of the terrace into some nettles below. This explained why the swear words were rather more distant than the scream. No doubt expecting some words of sympathy from me, he was surprised by my next question. 'Is there a snow leopard out there?' 'Oh yeah, several' came the sarcastic reply.

In the morning I relayed my story to the porters and the rest of our party who had been camped further down the hillside. It was met with a mixture of shock, excitement and scepticism. The porters, being very polite and eager to please, like all their wonderful fellow hill people in Nepal, accepted the truth of my assertions and helpfully pointed out various indentations in the soil as being possible paw marks, although others said they could just as easily have been from a number of other sources. We will never know.

Our party consisted of about a dozen people, half of whom were porters. Originally I had thought that having so many porters was a great indulgence and that the British members of the team should carry their fair share of the luggage, but I changed my mind about ten minutes after starting the trek. A typical day's walk involved ascending three or four thousand feet, then descending the same amount, then ascending again, up and down, up and down, over rough tracks, some of which clung to precipices, sometimes crossing rivers and streams by rope bridges. In the hills of Nepal nobody expresses distances in miles or kilometres, but in number of days' walk, because it can sometimes take a day just to cover a few miles.

I felt humiliated that that these small, spindly Nepalese men, recruited from various hill tribes, some barefoot and others wearing sandals, should be carrying heavy loads for days on end while I carried nothing more than a camera and a notepad. But I soon got over it. Exhaustion helps greatly in making sensible decisions about self-preservation. It was easy to persuade myself that this was a noble act enabling the porters to earn much-needed income; a similar argument, in fact, to that used by whites in apartheid South Africa to justify paying poverty level wages to their domestic servants. At the time of our visit, a porter earned about 16 rupees a day, equivalent to US$1.30.

I simply went with the flow and left the porters to take the strain. What was surprising was the way they took the strain. Everything was placed in a *doko* (a tapered cylindrical basket) that was carried on the porter's back but with the weight being taken on a strap over the forehead. As an experiment I tried to lift and carry an average weight *doko* and nearly yanked my head from its moorings while doing a backwards somersault, much to the amusement of the onlookers. The average weight carried by one porter was one *maund* (37kg) but a strong porter might carry up to two *maund*. No wonder that a sociologist had found in a survey of working age men that the lowest life expectancy was to be found among rickshaw drivers in Bangladesh and porters in Nepal.

There were no roads in this part of Nepal, so everything had to be carried by porters or pack animals. A few years previously a French adventurer named Michel Peissel had tried to prove that mini hovercraft could be used on the Kali Gandaki river, which explained why bits of broken and abandoned Western machinery were sometimes found incongruously strewn around the villages, but all he proved was that the Himalayas were not going to be tamed so easily.

The only other means of transport was by helicopter, and a few days previously I had made my first ever helicopter flight, courtesy of the Minister of Agriculture. The purpose of our mission to Nepal was to carry out a study that seemed doomed to failure before it started. Some years previously a Nepalese agricultural scientist had received specialist training in the UK in pomology, apple production. On his return to Nepal he had persuaded the government to support a major programme of encouraging farmers to plant apple orchards in certain parts of the country, particularly in the high hills. It was true that apples of the highest quality could be grown in these areas but, as was so often the case, no thought had been given to marketing. It was a common refrain; the technical challenge of successfully growing the crop overshadowed any consideration of finding a profitable market. Faced with a glut of high-quality apples languishing in parts of the inaccessible hills, but with no easy way of transporting them to Kathmandu and the other population centres, the Nepalese Ministry of Agriculture appealed to the British aid programme for help. The Mustang region, through which the Kali Gandaki flowed, was identified as the area where the problem was most acute.

Clearly there was not going to be any easy quick–fix solution to this problem short of building a road up the valley (very difficult terrain and therefore very costly) or bringing in thousands of rich Westerners to buy the apples. The latter solution became a partial reality some years later when trekking in Nepal became very popular and our route became part of the Annapurna Circuit. However, in the short term, we were left with more improbable scenarios to investigate, such as packing apples in containers to be carried by mule train for six days down to the nearest road for onward transport to major markets, by which time they would probably have been transformed from Red Delicious into red mush.

Another suggestion was that the apples could be made into

dried apple rings, which would have been much easier and cheaper to transport. It was argued that these could be sold to the growing band of trekkers as low weight food to carry with them. I calculated that if every trekker who entered the country at that time emptied his/her rucksack and filled it with dried apple rings, then 1% of the surplus would be utilised.

Compared to the feasibility study undertaken in Afghanistan, this was a small project and only warranted sending two 'experts' from the institute. The usual approach was to send one scientist and one economist. At that time, the Tropical Products Institute divided all its employees (who numbered in excess of 300) into three categories – scientists, economists and administrators. The term 'scientist' covered anyone with a qualification, very often a PhD, in any number of technical subjects related to agricultural production, storage or processing. The term 'economist' covered anyone with a background in economics, marketing or virtually any aspect of business. In the pecking order, scientists considered themselves to be superior to economists, while administrators were generally considered to be the lowest of the low because they had no opportunities to travel on projects and stayed glued to their desks in London. Everything changed some years later in the era of Margaret Thatcher, who had little or no interest in the aid programme except as an instrument of foreign policy, when an administrator was made the director of the whole institute.

One of the main roles of the economist on a team was to bring some semblance of commercial logic to the proceedings. There had been embarrassing examples in the past of scientists getting so immersed in their research that they lost all sense of reality. One example was a boffin who spent quite a lot of time developing a machine worthy of a Heath Robinson cartoon for dehusking coconuts. His eureka moment was spoilt when it was pointed out that the machine worked at 10% the rate of a man doing the same job and that, in any case, labour was cheap in coconut-producing countries. For their part the scientists viewed the economists as mealy-mouthed number crunchers, so putting the two together usually provided a reasonable balance. It also meant that the scientists, who, for all their higher degrees, were often illiterate in terms of being able to write a well-constructed and cogently argued report, were usually paired with someone with better report writing skills.

On this assignment I was working with Dr Keith Thompson, head of the institute's fruit and vegetable technology section. Apart from a facility for urinating while dropping over a precipice, he was also well qualified in the post-harvest characteristics of fruit. We set off on October 16th 1978. There were no direct flights to Kathmandu at that time, so we travelled via Tehran and Delhi. Inevitably, given the state of total chaos at Delhi airport in those days, combined with the policy of Royal Nepal Airlines of selling twice the number of tickets as seats, we arrived in Kathmandu half a day late. The first thing to do on arrival was to advance our watches by 15 minutes to accommodate the time difference between India and Nepal. The relationship between the two countries is sometimes characterised as that between a mouse and an elephant, but sometimes the mouse is eager to assert its independence and the time difference was a case in point.

Our local arrangements were being handled by the British embassy and an organisation called the Gurkha Reintegration Scheme (GRS), which existed to help former soldiers reintegrate into an agricultural and village-based way of life. The latter was a good deal more helpful to us than the former. I had already developed a mild loathing of British diplomats on the basis of previous experience in many countries, which was reinforced during several trips to Nepal over the next four years. Many embassy staff were arrogant and lazy while at the same time claiming that that they were desperately overworked. But if you only open the office between 8am and 2.30pm and take all UK and local public holidays, of course you are overworked in regular office hours because there are so few of them.

Perhaps things have improved now, but in the 1970s and 1980s, many British diplomatic staff dealt with everyone, no matter whether they were British or locals (with the possible exception of royalty and senior politicians) on the basis of total disdain. Some of the worst offenders were to be found in Kathmandu. One particular First Secretary affected an air of smelling a bad fish if you even gently suggested that he should read one of the files within his area of responsibility. It transpired that he was writing a book, which occupied a good deal of his work time, and he really didn't have time for anything so mundane as reading a file.

The usual round of briefing meetings had been set up for Keith and myself with the Ministry of Agriculture, other ministries, local agricultural research stations, the World Bank representative and the relevant United Nations offices, including the Food and Agriculture Organisation. The Nepalese ministries had the rare distinction of making even their Afghan equivalents appear to be models of bureaucratic excellence. A typical day in a Nepalese ministry officially began at 10am and ended at 4pm, but people would casually drift in at about 11 and drift away about 3. In between, of course, there was lunch, which could take a couple of hours, particularly if you had to go home to eat it. All this was extremely frustrating for a keen-as-mustard economist who still wanted to save the world, even though he was working on a project at this particular moment that almost certainly had no conceivable solution. Nevertheless, Keith and I were going to give it our best shot, so we religiously did as many meetings as possible in the time available.

At least we had the compensation of being in Kathmandu and could enjoy all the wonders of the city itself and the surrounding Kathmandu Valley with its Hindu temples, Buddhist stupas, pagodas, palaces, little yellow idols and all the rest of it. It's amazing how different people can visit the same place and have totally different opinions. I loved the mix of wonderful buildings and the hustle and bustle of the crowded alleyways and narrow streets. But we met some foreign tourists, particularly Americans and Germans, who could not see beyond the piles of filth lying around everywhere emitting horrible smells. One particular group of Americans in our hotel were on a three-week world tour (I joke not) and were spending a whole day and a half in Nepal, which they thought was far too long given the squalor and dilapidation of the place.

Some of the temples in the Kathmandu valley are famous for the profusion of Kama Sutra-style erotic carvings that adorn their outer walls. An excellent source of amusement is to position yourself with a good view of the tourists' faces and just watch the range of reactions. Most are amused and smile a lot, exchanging knowing looks with their partners. Others are shocked, while some are intrigued yet disbelieving that these positions are physically possible. On one occasion, a group of Catholic nuns got out of a mini-bus and made their way towards the temples. As they became aware of the erotic spectacle before them, most averted their eyes and rapidly made their way to the safer territory of a closer inspection of the prayer wheels, but one nun got out her binoculars and started making sketches in a notepad. The mind boggles.

The really exciting thing about this assignment was that we had to visit some of the most important areas of apple production in the high hills. In the first place, this meant a visit to Mustang, a district in West Central Nepal, on the Tibetan border, that had once been a major transit route but had lost that role after the Chinese invasion of Tibet in 1949, since when it had been a restricted area to Westerners until only a few years prior to our visit. The Minister of Agriculture was taking a personal interest in our mission and had decided that he would personally accompany us to Marfa Farm, a government agricultural station in Mustang, which was to be the start point of our investigations. We would be flown in the Minister's helicopter, firstly to Muktinath, a holy Hindu shrine only a few miles from the Tibetan border, where the Minister would worship at the temple of Jwala Mai, and then on to Marfa Farm. After appropriate celebrations, speeches and so on, the Minister would then fly back to Kathmandu, leaving Keith and myself to walk southwards to the town of Pokhara, a trek of seven days, allowing for numerous side trips to visit apple production areas along the way.

The helicopter flight from Kathmandu to Muktinath took only about one hour but enabled us to see as wide a range of fantastic sights as a boy from Uxbridge might expect to see in a lifetime. Leaving Kathmandu, at just over 4,000 ft, and flying to the west, we soon had a view of the great peaks of the central Nepalese Himalayas lined up in military order to our right – Manaslu (26,781 ft), Machhapuchhare (the magnificent fish-tail mountain, but only a tiddler at 22,956 ft), Annapurna (26,545 ft) and Dhaulagiri (26,811 ft). Behind us, in the far distance to the east, were Everest, local name Sagarmatha, (29,028 ft) and Kanchenjunga (28,208 ft). Nepal is home to nine of the world's 14 highest peaks.

I spent most of my first helicopter flight in open-mouthed amazement, but that did not matter too much because conversation was out of the question due to the deafening noise. I barely had time to be frightened except when I looked down at my feet, because the floor of the machine was see-through. Looking directly down is always more vertiginous than looking out to left or right, but I was repeatedly drawn back to the changing drama beneath my feet. It started with the urban scene of Kathmandu, then gave way to beautiful terraced hillsides that were so close I could almost touch them, then lush tropical vegetation where the monsoon deposits as much rainfall as is received by any place on the planet. After that came the snows and peaks of the main mountain range and finally, the arid relative flatness of the Plateau of Tibet in the rain shadow to the north with yaks grazing in the sunshine. Here was Muktinath at 12,000ft.

Unlike many members of my family, I am not a religious person. In fact, I think that religions have been responsible for many of the ills of the world and I am always ready to reinforce my prejudices with some further examples of the follies of the followers of the great religions. This is usually easiest in countries where two religions are found side by side, because competition invariably reinforces irrational hatreds, nearby Kashmir being a case in point. But even I have to admit that Nepal seems to have achieved an enviable peaceful coexistence between Hinduism and Buddhism, to the extent that many places of worship are shared.

Such examples are found all over the country and Muktinath is a case in point. Most Nepalese say they are Hindu, but perhaps it is because Buddha was born in their country, at Lumbini in the south, that they manage to be so tolerant. Maybe the Nepalese should send out aid missions to the religious hotspots of the world to teach them how to coexist and genuinely love thy neighbour.

Next stop was Marpha Farm, where the Minister and the helicopter took their leave of us. Here we met our Nepalese counterparts, who were to accompany us on our trek, and also two other Brits who were to be members of our party, who had arrived via the STOL airport a little further up the valley at Jomsom. One was a horticulturist, who would be useful to have on the trip, and the other was a Second Secretary from the embassy.

At Marpha Farm we met Nepalese civil servants who were a different type from the indolent ministry men of Kathmandu. Now we were among agriculturalists, horticulturalists and other technical specialists who were trying hard, with minimal resources, to provide a useful advisory service to the farmers of the area, who were mostly scratching a living from tiny plots of terraced land precariously clinging to hillsides and in constant danger of collapse from the forces of erosion.

One of the senior staff was Pasang Sherpa, whose amazingly varied background included a period studying viticulture in France. Apart from his more conventional activities, Pasang had built a small distillery and produced some very fine spirits from local raw materials. He had seen it all before and was, correctly, very sceptical about the chances of success of our mission, but still maintained an outward show of great hospitality and courtesy. A couple of weeks later, in Kathmandu, I was privileged to be shown Pasang's priceless collection of Tibetan books and scrolls, some dating back centuries, which he had accumulated over many years of living in the border area.

Madan Rai was a young horticulturalist who would accompany us on our trek to the south. He knew the area intimately and would take us to the apple-growing areas, introduce us to farmers and act as guide, interpreter and general organiser of food, accommodation and porters. If anyone deserved the title of expert it was Madan, but that was not the way of things at that time.

Our route started off by following the Kali Gandaki River which, at this point, flows almost due south on its way to meet the Ganges. With Dhaulagiri to the west and Annapurna to the east, it forms the deepest gorge in the world, reaching a depth of about 18,000 ft at the maximum. The Grand Canyon, itself a staggering mile deep down to the Colorado River on its floor, could be fitted three times over into the depth of the Kali Gandaki gorge.

In the valley and the nearby hills there were scattered villages and farming communities. The houses were very basic, without any modern amenities such as electricity or toilet facilities, but the overall appearance was very attractive, enhanced by monasteries and temples at regular intervals. In years to come this would become one of the most famous trekking routes in the world and become overrun with Westerners. Trekking lodges, restaurants and other facilities expected by Western tourists, even when they are 'roughing it', would be built, but few of these things existed in 1978.

Our accommodation alternated between camping in tents, with or without the company of snow leopards, and sleeping on the floors of houses along the way. It was by no means unusual for the village headman or one of the other villagers to invite our party to stay the night and to offer food. In such cases we simply laid out our sleeping bags in the family's communal sleeping area. This was the customary courtesy to travellers, and I experienced exactly the same level of hospitality some years later when I worked in the hill areas of eastern Nepal. Yet again it was a case of those who have least offering the most. Of course, we insisted on making some payment, but it was never expected or requested by our hosts.

Food was a disappointment. My favourite eating-place in west London, where I lived at the time, was Monty's Nepalese restaurant in South Ealing. Monty Shresthra had moved from Kathmandu to London some years previously and established his first restaurant, which although rather small and pokey, soon achieved an excellent reputation. I had innocently imagined that in Nepal, I would be sitting down to chicken tikka or lamb prasand each evening, with a side order of brinjal bhajee. How wrong could I be. The food in rural Nepal bears almost no resemblance to Monty's menu. Chicken tikka masala is certainly not available. The regular diet, meal after meal, day after day, is *dall bat* (rice and lentils). Meat is an unaffordable luxury for most people and, in any case, for religious or cultural reasons, many people are vegetarian or semi-vegetarian. The complexities of who can eat what are mind-boggling. Some people will eat chicken but no other meat, others are allowed to eat pigeon, some will eat water buffalo and a few will even eat beef if the animal has died of natural causes which is why, in some parts of Nepal, there are occasional supplies of beef from cattle which have reportedly fallen over precipices, although in reality the meat has probably been brought up from India by Muslim traders. But all these fine distinctions were largely academic in most parts of rural Nepal, because meat was often not available, particularly when out on trek.

On one occasion, in eastern Nepal, when the thought of yet more *dall bat* made me heave, I offered a reward for some meat. Later I was sitting in near darkness in the tiny house where we were staying, with my eyes smarting from the smoke of the fire set in the middle of the main room, when a triumphant villager appeared holding a bloody dead animal with what looked like quills sticking out of its back, presumably a porcupine, and I was asked how I would like it cooked. I paid the man but declined the feast.

At least rice and lentils are highly nutritious. Although I found the diet horribly repetitive, the Nepalese seemed oblivious to the boredom factor; even when they travel outside the country to places like the UK, where the choice of foods available is enormous, they still crave for their daily dose of *dall bat*.

A couple of years later my wife and I inadvertently gave Madan Rai the culinary surprise of his life. He was attending a training course in the UK and came to stay at our house in London. He had just been explaining to us that he had found a wholesale outlet where he could buy rice in bulk at a good price when my wife served dessert – rice pudding. Madan's face was a picture. Astonishment turned to helpless laughter. I suppose it would be the equivalent of a British person when abroad being served a dessert of potato in hot, sugary milk.

The main culinary highlight of the trek was a fried egg. It's amazing how simple pleasures are the best. After a few days of a diet of *dall bat* (supplemented by enormous quantities of excellent apples which we were given as presents at every stop along the way) I was walking along the trail one day, fantasising about items on Monty's menu, when we came across an ordinary village house with a sign outside saying 'Meena and Beena's Bar and Grill'. At first I dismissed this as a mirage, but on closer inspection there really was a little café with a couple of tables and a few chairs; and joy of joy, they had some eggs. Two enterprising sisters had seen the future and invested all their money in establishing a little eating-house to supply the growing number of trekkers. I hope they became rupee millionaires over the following years. I also hope that their knowledge about hygiene improved because, like most of their countrymen at the time, their kitchen, utensils and hands were filthy. This problem explains why most Westerners have regular bouts of 'Delhi belly' in Nepal, but all that mattered nothing on this occasion set against the euphoria of eating a fried egg.

The variety of drinks available was rather better. We had to resist the temptation to drink from the inviting mountain streams in the knowledge that goats, yaks or perhaps even snow leopards had used these torrents as a toilet further upstream. Instead we drank *chai* (tea), often bought from the ever-present little teashops along the route, and Coca Cola. There are two Western companies that I always quote when speaking at training courses on marketing in developing countries – Singer (as in sewing machines) and Coca Cola. In the 1970s both products were found in nearly every corner of the globe. I can't think of anywhere I have been, including the remotest hill areas of Nepal, where Coca Cola was not available. The only exceptions would be countries such as the USSR, where it was banned, but in that case Pepsi filled the breach. At home in England I avoid fizzy, bottled drinks like the plague, but they have been lifesavers in various remote parts of the world, particularly in the days before bottled water became ubiquitous.

I had my first experience of two other types of drinks on this trip, Tibetan tea and *rakshi*. Tibetan tea, a mixture of tea, yaks' butter and salt , is the foulest concoction that has ever passed my lips. In fact it barely did pass my lips. During my first evening at Marpha Farm, Pasang Sherpa bet me that I could not drink a small cup of it. Accepting the challenge, I raised the cup to just below my nose and the smell was so diabolical that I had to suppress a strong urge to throw up on the spot. Not wishing to appear like a wimpish Westerner I forced the evil liquid to my lips, but after the first little sip I had to admit defeat, much to the delight of Pasang and the assembled company.

Rakshi, on the other hand, became a regular feature of my diet. It's a spirit distilled from barley or fruits, according to the availability of raw materials and the preferences of the makers. Many houses have their own still, so the variety of types and qualities of the product is very wide. The real surprise was the start time for drinking, usually about 10am. The regular pattern of our days on the trek was to rise at daybreak and start walking after a quick cup of *chai*. Given the terrain, we were tired and in need of a rest and food by about 9 or 10am, often coinciding with a visit to a group of apple producers and an invitation to take food with them. It was customary to finish the meal with some *rakshi*, which greatly helped us to face the next ascent or descent of 3,000 ft or more. Just as I had become accustomed to stewed rhubarb for breakfast in Afghanistan, so I now started salivating like a Pavlov dog for my daily dose of *rakshi* at about 9 am.

Another feature of the local way of life to which it was necessary to become accustomed was the lack of bathrooms. I could cope with washing in mountain streams, but it took rather longer to get used to the toilet arrangements. Occasionally we would be directed towards a cesspit, but these places were so indescribably awful that it was a relief to be told in a particular village that we were to use the nearby fields.

One morning I was going about my business having found a suitably sheltered place out of sight of the village and with a few trees for cover. I am not a naturally good squatter, perhaps being tall makes it that bit more difficult, but I could usually endure the discomfort for the required time, except on this particular day. Captivated by the magnificent mountain scenery around me, I did not notice that my toilet roll was doing what toilet rolls do on an incline, rolling. I just managed to grab the last bit of paper as the remainder of the roll made a very impressive streamer over the side of the terrace bank in front of me. The only thing to do was to laboriously re-roll the paper in the reverse direction, all the time, of course, in the squatting position.

I was so engrossed in my task that I only noticed the party of French trekkers at the last moment. I thought I had positioned myself well away from the nearest trail, but I had obviously miscalculated as they were passing only a short distance away. This had all the hallmarks of being my most embarrassing moment since being caught short with a bout of dysentery in a Tehran street in 1971. Now I crouched down even further than previously in the vain hope that the French would not see me or my rather fetching pink streamer.

Eventually the babble of voices died away and I returned to my task until the paper was all re-rolled. Throughout this episode

I had been trying to ignore the escalating and searing pain in my calves and thighs but, to make matters worse, I had now been in the squat position for so long that I was locked into place by cramp. I will not provide enlightenment on how I extricated myself from this predicament, but it was not a pretty sight.

The next humiliation came later that same day at the hands of the porters. We had to take off our shoes and socks to cross a stream. The first sign of trouble was a gasp of amazement from one of the porters. I would be the first to admit that my feet are not my best feature, but people don't usually stop in horror when confronted with them. But English size 13 was something this porter had not seen before and the spectacle seemed worthy of calling over his fellow porters to have a look. Not content with inflicting this indignity, they hailed passing individuals and families who took it in turns to place their feet alongside mine and usually found that one of mine equalled at least two of theirs.

There was no malice in this; it was just another opportunity to smile and laugh, something that the hill people of Nepal seemed to be doing all the time. I noticed this repeatedly in my travels in Nepal over the next few years. No matter whether it was the Thakali people in Mustang or the Sherpas, Rais, Gurungs, Newars or any other group of hill people, they all seemed delighted to meet strangers and to have an almost constant smile on their faces, male and female, young and old. As we approached each village little children would come rushing to great us with hands clasped, palms together in front of their faces in the traditional greeting, saying 'Namaste' and sometimes combining this with the presentation of a garland of marigolds.

How is it that people who have so little seem to be more cheerful than people who have so much? Of course it is not that simple. There are plenty of examples of groups of poor people around the world; the street dwellers of Mumbai or the shantytown inhabitants of Nairobi spring to mind, who seem as miserable as one would expect them to be. But there are so many others who give the appearance of being very happy, although they have very few material possessions, no reserves of wealth for a rainy day and virtually no access to the education, health and other services that Westerners take for granted.

It is not a novel question, some might say it is clichéd, but I have often reflected on this seeming conundrum. Is it to do with genes, family life, culture, religion, rural versus urban, the pressures of Western living, different levels of expectation or what? To ask the same question in reverse, why do many Americans and Europeans, myself included, appear to be so relatively miserable? In spite of our cars, household goods, social services and high incomes, we look more miserable and treat each other with much less respect. But it is obviously not poverty that puts a smile on peoples' faces. The Japanese manage to be rich, yet still full of smiles, and they treat each other with great respect. National or ethnic stereotyping is obviously fraught with danger, not least because there are always exceptions that prove the rule (there are some Germans with a sense of humour) but such behavioural patterns do seem to exist.

The highs and lows of the trek continued, both literally and figuratively. The lows occurred on those days when I felt ill with a bout of fever or stomach trouble and knew I had no option but to walk all day long. Thankfully, those days were greatly outnumbered by the highs when I had to keep asking myself if this wonderful adventure, amongst such fascinating people and the best scenery in the world, was a dream or not. Exhilaration and exhaustion went hand in hand on this trip, but the former always eclipsed the latter.

In the interests of balance, I should also point out that Nepal contains a couple of the worst places in the world that I have ever visited. One of them is Biratnagar, the second largest town in Nepal outside the Kathmandu Valley, which is located in the south-east corner of the country close to the Indian border. It often comes as a surprise to some foreigners to learn that the southern strip of Nepal, known as the Terai, is a hot, flat, low-lying area which is an extension of the north Indian plain; a sort of Nepalese East Anglia. It could hardly be in greater physical contrast to the hill areas, and the differences are reinforced by the fact that the local population are North Indians by background, quite different in appearance and culture from the people of the hill tribes although many of the latter have been attracted to migrate southwards by the high fertility and relatively easy farming of the Terai. Biratnagar is a dirty, dusty, crowded place without any of the redeeming features of Kathmandu. It totally lacks charm or at least it did the last time I visited the place in 1980. On that occasion I counted 29 electricity power cuts in one day, which should be worthy of an entry in the Guinness Book of Records.

We continued down the Kali Gandaki valley and then parted company from the river to follow the trail to Pokhara, a town located about 120 miles to the west of Kathmandu. Seeing and hearing motorised vehicles again seemed like a real intrusion upon the peaceful splendour in which we had been living for the past seven days. It was only at this point, in retrospect, that I realised that this had been the first time in my life that I had experienced an existence without motor transport. Even when I had lived for 18 months in rural Africa I had seldom been out of earshot of vehicles and as a Londoner, I had spent most of my life in very close proximity to virtually every form of wheeled transport known to man. It dawned on me what life had been like for all people in the world as recently as my own grandparents' generation. Of course, like most Westerners, I contribute to the tyranny of the motorcar by being a driver and regular road user, but the lack of noise, pollution and roadside danger during the trek was an eye-opener in terms of realising what we have sacrificed.

Back in Kathmandu we proceeded with the inevitable round of meetings and I, as the marketing man on the team, spent a good deal of time pursuing one of my favourite pastimes of visiting markets and traders to get an understanding of how the fruit trade was organised. We now had a reasonable grasp of the problems faced by the apple growers in Mustang, but our Nepalese hosts at the Ministry of Agriculture also wanted us to extend our investigations to the neighbouring districts of Manang and Dolpa, which were located on the Tibetan border on either side of Mustang. Apparently, the apple-planting frenzy had also taken hold in these districts, again encouraged by the Ministry. If Mustang was remote, then these places were even more inaccessible, both being to the north of the main mountain range and even more days' walk from the nearest road. We had no more time to do another trek, so the only alternative was to take a trip in a whirlybird.

Hiring a helicopter in Nepal proved to be much easier than renting a car in the USA. This was one of the intriguing little quirks of being a civil servant working for the Ministry of Overseas Development. When I needed to hire a car in the USA the following year on official business, I was told that it was out of the question because no budget for car rental existed for someone of my grade and therefore I would have to take a bus or train, neither of which was available on the particular routes in question. Try explaining that to someone in the USA who is giving you directions on how to reach their office. Such nonsense hastened the day when I would say goodbye to the British Civil Service. But when it came to hiring a helicopter in Nepal, at hundreds of times the cost of renting a car in the USA, no problem, the man at the embassy had some money left in his helicopter budget, so Keith and I spent a whole day flying into and out of remote parts of Manang and Dolpa districts.

We reported to Kathmandu airport at 7am and met Mr Singh, our pilot. He explained that we would need to refuel at least twice during the day and that the only refuelling stations were located to the south of the main mountain range. Since most of the villages we needed to visit were close to the Tibetan border, this meant that we would spend the whole day criss-crossing the part of the Himalayas consisting of Annapurna I to IV, Nilgiri, Manaslu, Dhaulagiri I to VI and several other peaks.

From Kathmandu we flew halfway across Nepal for a refuelling stop at the lowland town of Nepalganj on the border with India and then northwards, round the back of the Dhaulagiri Range, to a village in Dolpa. I was now getting rather blasé about this helicopter flying business. I felt like an old hand. But my sanguine attitude changed abruptly and dramatically as a result of a conversation with Mr Singh while we were preparing for the next leg of our journey. 'I expect you have flown around these mountains thousands of times', I said cheerily. 'Oh no, this is my first time', he answered, equally cheerily. 'Ha ha,' I said, playing along with his little game of frightening me. This verbal cat and mouse continued for a while until I realised that he was actually telling the truth. It transpired that he had been a helicopter pilot in the Indian Air Force somewhere in north India where the highest hill was about the size of the Taj Mahal and had started employment in Kathmandu only the previous month. But he was having 'a spiffing good time' in his new job and I wasn't to worry about a thing.

I felt like the cat in 'Tom and Jerry' when he has just been poleaxed by another misfortune. The confidence drained out of me and I was overcome by a sudden urge for a very large glass of *rakshi*. I tried to weigh up my options. They seemed to boil down to a choice between getting back into the helicopter or setting off on a seven-day trek over high altitude passes in freezing temperatures without any suitable clothing, footwear or food. The decision was a close-run thing, which I mulled over for some time, with pros and cons on both sides, but getting back into the helicopter just won.

I regretted this decision almost immediately after take-off. Mr Singh handed me a map and shouted out instructions over the noise of the machine. 'We have to find a way through the mountains to our next destination but our ceiling is 17,000 ft and so I want you to count the contours on the map and tell me if we can make it'. I looked at his face very carefully, waiting for him to erupt into laughter and say he was only joking, but his face just had the look of a man who was really enjoying himself. He motioned to me to get on with my task. Here we were, surrounded by peaks of 26,000ft and over, and I now had the responsibility of deciding whether or not we flew straight into the side of a snow-capped mountain. I made a determined effort to stop trembling sufficiently to read the map, but the contours were so close together that they were almost solid brown lines.

I immersed myself in the task and laboriously counted the contours along each stage of the journey. At one point I found myself counting 17,050, and a little alarm bell rang in my head. With commendable British aplomb I mentioned this fact to Mr Singh. 'Oh lummy', he said. I don't know the technical term for a U-turn in a helicopter, perhaps it's something like the Australian expression 'A screaming uey', but that is what we did in this particular Himalayan valley. I also don't know the exact dimensions of the turning circle of a helicopter, but I do know that our rotor blades seemed virtually to touch the ice wall on either side. 'That was fun', said Mr Singh.

We proceeded in this manner for the rest of the day. I noticed that some of the villages were not named on the map and pointed this out to Mr Singh. 'Perhaps, they weren't there when the map was drawn,' he replied. I looked down at the date of the map. There it was, printed in clear black type – 1926; the map was over 50 years old. By this stage I was past caring and just went back to counting contours.

Apart from the physical danger, something else was worrying me about this particular trip. I was disturbed by the way we were dropping in on these villages like men from Mars. They were not forewarned of our arrival because there was no means of contacting them in advance. The first they knew of it was the sound of the helicopter, followed by the disembarkation of beings from another planet who started asking a lot of questions about apples before disappearing as quickly as they had arrived. At least in Mustang we had turned up at each village on foot and had sufficient time fully to explain what we were doing. I feared that our intervention might be interpreted by the people as a sign that the outside world was desperate to buy their apples and would go to the lengths of arriving by helicopter to make their purchases whereas, in reality, there was little chance that the villagers would find a market for their apple surpluses.

Keith and I completed our work in Nepal and returned to London to work on our report. We were under pressure from various sides. The Nepalese let it be known that King Birendra himself wanted a major horticultural project in the three districts because the growing of subsistence crops like rice and wheat could never be sufficient to support the population. Marketing and transport problems were brushed aside on the basis that roads would be built in the future or airfreight transport would become cheaper and more plentiful, neither of which was likely to happen in the foreseeable future. We ended up writing a fudged document, a typical aid sector cop out, saying that more studies would be needed before full proposals could be made.

Apart from the narrow problems of apple marketing, this experience of carrying out a study in Nepal highlighted a broader dilemma of working in the international aid sector. There are some places in the world where human existence at a reasonable standard of living is hardly viable. Even if all other factors of what is sometimes called the 'enabling environment ' (good government, lack of war and internal strife, sensible economic policies and so on) are in place, which they never are, the other problems (difficult terrain, transport difficulties, lack of water and other resources, population pressure and many, many others) are just so great that life without subsidy is not really possible. This applies to many of the hill areas of Nepal. Tourism and hydroelectric power offer some potential for increasing incomes, but most people have to rely on agriculture.

During the period from 1978 to 1981 I was involved in various projects in Nepal aimed at developing the agricultural potential of the hills, particularly through cash crops such as tea, spices, medicinal herbs, fruits and vegetables. The aid agencies bent over backwards trying to help, often getting in each other's way in the process, but the bottom line was that there were too many people trying to squeeze an existence out of a confined, albeit beautiful, space which had very few resources. To make matters worse, the political environment became more unstable in the early years of the 21st century resulting from Crown Prince Dipendra's decision in 2001 to wipe out most of the royal family with a machine gun.

After the royal massacre, the ruling classes looked around for someone with royal blood who was still alive. This turned out to be the murdered King Birendra's brother, Gyanendra. The new king dissolved parliament and Nepal's fledgling democracy was put on hold. Even political moderates expressed their dissatisfaction in riots, and Maoist guerrillas went from strength to strength in many rural areas. The economic effects were dire. The country is heavily reliant on tourism, but many trekkers and climbers were robbed or endured short-term kidnapping. Later, the Maoists entered the political mainstream and they have had periods in and out of government. The economy continued to be depressed. A further crushing blow to the people of Nepal and the tourist industry was delivered in April 2015 when a 7.8 magnitude earthquake struck Kathmandu and the surrounding areas, leaving 8.000 dead and millions homeless.

So, what to do with Nepal? Leave it to its fate, admitting that it may not be really viable as a country, or hang in there and try to help? For me, it has to be the latter. I don't mind if a little bit of my taxes goes towards propping up a way of life that deserves to be preserved. Nepal is one of the poorest countries in Asia, exceeding in per capita income only Afghanistan and one or two others. Apart from tourism, the Nepalese economy is heavily dependent on foreign aid and remittances from overseas workers. The 28 million people (2018 data) have few realistic opportunities for significant development, particularly those scratching an income from tiny plots of land in the hills. The country is likely to need help for the long term. Of course, aid has to be wisely spent, properly targeted and made conditional upon certain reforms, but there is little alternative but to admit the inevitable.

Nepal postscript, January 2018

Forty years later, I am still a regular customer of Monty's restaurant, now moved a short distance to Ealing Broadway, and enjoy chatting with Monty Shrestra about the ups and downs of life in Nepal. On this occasion a new waiter, in his early 20s, showed us to our table and I took the opportunity to ask him where he was from. After saying that I would not know the place, it transpired that he was from Mustang and he was delighted to find that I had visited the area long before he was born. He then asked a question, out of the blue, which stopped me in my tracks. 'Were you anything to do with the apple project of that time?' When I said that I had played a small part, he then delighted me by saying that the new 'Jeep road' connecting Jomsom and Muktinath with the road network further south had enabled apples and other products to be marketed in the population centres. This had transformed the incomes of many families.

Whether or not our report all those years ago had any effect on the decision to build a dirt road I will never know, but it thrilled me that some communities were benefiting from their new-found source of wealth. It vindicated those who had proceeded with apple tree planting in the 1970s in the hope that one day it would transform lives.

CHAPTER 7

ROUND THE WORLD WITH
DESICCATED COCONUT, 1978

One of my unique contributions to Third World development was being the proud author of a 90-page report entitled 'The World Market for Desiccated Coconut', published by the Tropical Products Institute in 1979. Those of you who would like to buy a copy will be disappointed because it is now out of print, but if you are desperate for a good read I understand that copies are available in the library of TPI's successor organisation, the Natural Resources Institute.

As far as I'm concerned, desiccated coconut is a serious subject worthy of serious discussion, but it usually raises a few titters when mentioned in general conversation. The reaction of family and friends to different agricultural commodities is interesting. If you say your work relates to wheat in Afghanistan or tea in Nepal, the reaction is generally low key with a serious nod or two. If you say you are working on bananas in the Windward Islands you get a surprised look and a few sniggers. Mention that you are doing an in-depth project on desiccated coconut and it immediately evokes guffaws and John McEnroe style outbursts of, 'You cannot be serious'. Worse still, in later years my work related to cucumbers in Ukraine. I resisted all mention of the subject.

One friend in London in the late 1970s was absolutely convinced that I was a British spy. She knew that I was working for the British government (true), that I had signed the Official Secrets Act (true) and that my visit to any country usually coincided with a coup, invasion or some other disorder (often true). Putting two and two together, she came up with MI5. She took me quietly aside at one party and said, 'Look Stephen, I realise what kind of work you are involved in but surely you could come up with a more plausible cover story for a trip round the world than a project on desiccated coconut'.

Strange but true, I really did spend six months of my life working on this riveting subject. Let me persuade you that desiccated coconut really is fascinating by offering a few snippets from the report quoted above. No wait, don't turn the page – it really is interesting. For example, world trade in desiccated coconut in 1977 amounted to about 130,000 tons, which required about 1 billion coconuts to be used as the raw material – that's an awful lot of coconuts. The major producers were the Philippines and Sri Lanka, with several other tropical locations producing smaller amounts. Most desiccated coconut was exported to Europe and the USA, but the country with the highest per capita consumption was Australia, partly due to its obsession with a rather hideous desiccated coconut encrusted cake called a Lamington. One of the largest industrial users in Europe was Mars, with its Bounty bars, consuming more than 5,000 tons of the stuff each year in its factories in Slough in the UK and Veghel in the Netherlands. The connection between coconut palms in beautiful tropical locations and Slough is a little difficult to get your head round, but the link exists nevertheless. Production of this commodity has to be carried out in quite large factories, equipped with expensive machinery such as sterilizers and in very hygienic conditions, otherwise you risk killing your customers with salmonella poisoning. Many trading companies in New York, London, Rotterdam, Singapore and elsewhere made a good living from buying, selling and speculating (yes, speculating) on this commodity. See what I mean? Absolutely fascinating.

When my boss at the institute told me that my next project was to be a feasibility study into establishing a new desiccated coconut factory in the New Hebrides in the South Pacific, I could hardly believe my luck. Delicious images of South Sea maidens dancing the hula came to mind, encouraged by memories of the film 'Mutiny on the Bounty'. Quite false images as it turned out, because the people of the New Hebrides are Melanesians rather than Polynesians, but never mind, the idea of swanning around the South Sea Islands seemed highly attractive.

The institute's usual 'dream team' for a smaller project of a scientist and an economist was assembled. The scientist was Dr Ron Harris, who would be responsible for all the processing, packaging, storage and other technical aspects of the study. I was the economist, responsible for assessing the worldwide market opportunities for this product (my work would also be separately written up and published in the report mentioned earlier) and for carrying out the financial analysis. We would also need agricultural expertise from someone experienced in coconut plantation production but that would be readily available from among the plethora of expatriate agricultural officers who were resident in the New Hebrides.

In some ways Ron was typical of the senior scientists at the institute in that he had a PhD and considerable experience in many parts of the world in his chosen specialist subject area, which was oilseeds. But in other ways he was atypical. He was more of a jack-the-lad character. He liked a drink or several, smoked non-stop, even during meals and in lifts, had an eye for the girls and was not noted for undue exertion at work. That's not to say that he was lazy but that he aimed for a high level of achievement with the minimum of effort. An example of this was his generosity in allowing me to write the greater part of our final report.

Ron prided himself on never spending time in the UK in the horrible winter months of January and February by always managing to arrange a work trip to somewhere hot and exotic. Needless to say our trip to the South Pacific took place during January and February.

As the team leader, Ron planned our trip meticulously. By a happy coincidence all the places we needed to visit were desirable locations, at least compared to some of the hellholes it was possible to visit on institute business. Ron persuaded our superiors that we needed to make a study visit to the Philippines to see a couple of the large factories that were equipped with cutting-edge desiccated coconut technology. This would necessitate stopovers in Singapore on the way to Manila and Hong Kong on the way to our next destination, Australia. Apart from the fact that flights to the New Hebrides left from Brisbane, we also needed to visit Australia to assess the market opportunities for a potential new supplier. From the New Hebrides, Ron would return to the UK but I would continue round the world to the USA to visit traders, confectionary companies and other major users of the product to get a handle on the market in the biggest consuming country in the world. A little later I would also make a market research visit around Europe to carry out the same tasks. In total I visited 10 countries on my round-the-world journey, and it did take about 80 days.

The benefit of a short stopover in Singapore in 1978 was that it enabled us to see a little of the remaining architectural charm of the place before the entire island was converted into a gigantic modern shopping centre. We also dined out in a genuine street restaurant before these were sanitised and relocated to special sites. I suppose the government of Singapore has done a good job in providing higher incomes for 3 million people squeezed into a tiny space but, not being a keen shopper, I have found very little of interest in my subsequent visits. For my money, Hong Kong beats Singapore hands down for interest value, at least it did until more recent confrontations with the Chinese government. I am also very suspicious of any busybody state authority that passes laws, which are enforced in Singapore, on chewing gum use and flushing urinals in men's public toilets.

In the Philippines we were the guests of the Philippine Coconut Authority and the Philippine Association of Desiccators. You may laugh but coconut products (coconut oil, copra and desiccated coconut) actually constituted the main export sector of the Philippine economy at that time and employed vast numbers of people. The British tend to think of coconuts as the target for wooden balls at a fairground coconut shy but in some parts of the world, in economic terms, they are as important as coffee is to Brazil or tea is to India.

On our journeys to visit the factories, passing through the slums on the outskirts of Manila and the countryside of south Luzon, we got an impression of the great disparities in wealth between our very helpful and Americanised hosts in the business community and the great mass of the population. It was no surprise in later years to find that vast numbers of Filipino migrant workers were always to be found in the Middle East and anywhere else in the world that offered employment at more than the pittance income levels prevailing in the Philippines.

During our stay in Manila a kindly British diplomat invited us to his home for dinner and I was thinking of revising my opinion about members of his profession until he made this telling admission after a few too many glasses of wine: 'You know, after thirty tears in the diplomatic service, I have to admit that I really don't like coloured people'. Where do they find them?

I was enjoying Ron's company on our trip so far, with the single exception of his smoking habit. He would always light up in a crowded car or taxi and his capacity for smoking in restaurants, not only between courses but also while eating, was unusual even in those days. On the flight from Hong Kong to Sydney he developed another little habit that looked as if it might also prove to be life threatening. He started reading extracts out loud from a book entitled 'Let Stalk Strine' by Afferbeck Lauder. This book was described as a lexicon of the Australian language, but it could be a red rag to a bull when read out loud to the very people who were being made fun of.

'Here's a good one Stephen!' Ron shouted out over the noise

of the aeroplane's engines and across the crowded rows of seats that separated us in Economy Class. 'Egg Nishner – a mechanical device for cooling the air in a room'. Ron dissolved into helpless laughter. A couple of minutes later, 'What about this one, dimension – the usual response to thenk you or thenk smite'. Ron continued in this vein for some time and was laughing so much that he was totally oblivious to the rising rage among our fellow passengers. Even the Quantas stewards, were beginning to get annoyed. I was busy looking out of the window and pretending not to listen.

I half expected to be refused entry to Australia, but the pilot had obviously not bothered to radio ahead to warn the immigration authorities to keep the Pommie smartarses out. Mind you, Ron was still doing his best to alienate the entire population of Oz by continuing to read out extracts as we disembarked. At the first opportunity I clapped my hand over his mouth and made him promise to read the book only in the privacy of his hotel room and, even then, to do it silently.

The next part of our Australian initiation was more alarming. We had arrived in Sydney in the middle of a heatwave and after checking into our hotel, our first priority was to start sampling the celebrated local cold beers in a nearby bar. We rushed in, ordered two beers and sat down on stools at the bar in eager anticipation. The barmaid put two glasses of beer down on the bar and Ron explained that there was a mistake because he wanted bottled beer, not draught. At this moment the world stood still. The bar became hushed and the muscular barmaid fixed Ron with an icy stare before picking up his glass and hurling it with great force into the sink, where it smashed into a hundred pieces. With great deliberation she then took a bottle of beer from the cold shelf and removed the top with her teeth, all the while maintaining her gaze on an increasingly uncomfortable Ron, before banging the bottle down on the bar

We sat on our stools like naughty schoolboys, trying not to whimper and taking occasional sips of beer. I took the opportunity to make furtive glances around the bar, being very careful to avoid eye contact with any living thing, including the Alsatian in the corner. I now understood why a female Australian relative on a recent visit to England had reacted with great alarm when my wife and I had suggested going for a drink in a local pub. Bars in Australia at this time were intimidating places and women (and perhaps Englishmen) did not enter unless there was a specific notice outside saying that they could be admitted. The only woman in this bar was the barmaid, who was even more ferocious than her customers, which was saying something. The bar was a place to get drunk; there was sawdust on the floor and tiles on the walls, and everything would be hosed down at closing time. The contrast with a welcoming English pub was total. Ron and I finished our beers and edged out the door.

This experience seemed to reinforce the prejudiced view about the stereotypical, abusive Aussie, always complaining about whingeing Poms. But beware of first impressions, because every other experience during the following week was completely at odds with this narrow-minded view. I discovered that nearly all Australians are scrupulously polite and will go out of their way to be helpful.

Sydney was a mixed bag of experiences. The beauty of Sydney harbour, with bridge and opera house, was in contrast to the more seedy parts of town where there were a lot of down-and-outs roaming the streets and sleeping rough, more it seemed than in London at the same time, although that would change in later years. Flying visits to Melbourne, Geelong, Bendigo (to visit 'rellies') and Brisbane followed before Ron and I took an Air Pacific flight to the New Hebrides via the French colony of New Caledonia.

It all looks quite close on an atlas page of the Pacific Ocean, but if you set off from Brisbane in a north-easterly direction you don't bump into the New Hebrides for about 1,000 miles. The islands themselves, numbering about 80 in total, are heavily forested, mountainous and volcanic, and spread out over more than 800 miles in a north-south direction. The New Hebrides were very different from anything I had experienced before. The people and their way of life were slightly reminiscent of parts of rural Africa, but there were also many differences, and these were reinforced by the most bizarre form of government I have ever come across – in fact it was completely bonkers.

Today the country is known as Vanuatu, having ditched its previous very colonial-sounding name, given by Captain Cook, on gaining independence in 1980. So when Ron and I visited in 1978 we were witnessing the death throes of the colonial regime. But it was a very unusual colonial arrangement because the New Hebrides (or Nouvelles-Hebrides, according to your choice) was a joint colony of the United Kingdom and France. In fact, it was officially known as the Condominium of the New Hebrides. This terminology led to a good deal of confusion on my visit to the USA. When I said I had been staying in the Condominium of the New Hebrides, it transpired that Americans thought I had visited an apartment block in the South Pacific rather than a group of islands. Further confusion reigned when I explained that the Condominium had dozens of coconut plantations and was planning to build a desiccated coconut factory.

At the time of our visit the total population of the New Hebrides numbered about 100,000 people, so if you had collected them all together they would have fitted into one large football stadium. This small number of people, some of whom were leading lives which would once have been described as primitive before that word became non-PC, must have been the most over-governed population in the world at the time. The British and the French had created a monster of a political system. Unable to compromise on one system, they had duplicated nearly everything. There were French courts and British courts, French prisons and British prisons, a French Ministry of Education and a British Ministry of Education, a French Resident Commissioner and a British Resident Commissioner, not to mention French District Agents and British District Agents in each of the major islands.

On arrival at the airport of the capital, Port-Vila, you actually had to make a choice between which judicial system you elected to be bound by during your stay, so that if you transgressed they would know which courts to take you to and which prisons to lock you up in. Presumably this was a fairly straightforward choice for British and French visitors, but making such a selection must have been mystifying for nationals from most other countries in the world.

As if two parallel bureaucratic systems were not enough, a third tier was being created in the run-up to independence. This was known as the New Hebrides government and consisted of appointed individuals who were being trained to take over when the French and British departed. Inevitably, there were deep divisions between the various local groups, who had very different ideas about what should happen in the future.

Can you imagine trying to explain this system of government in 1978 to one of the inhabitants of the islands? 'Well Mr Ravutia it's like this. You owe allegiance to the Queen of England and to the President of France'. (Apparently the fact that their photos were usually shown alongside each other led many New Hebrideans to think that Elizabeth and Giscard d'Estaing were married). 'They each have representatives who live in Port-Vila and those representatives have district agents who live on your island and you must obey what they say. Of course, there is also the Hon. Mr Kalsakau, who is Chief Minister of the New Hebrides Government, based in Port-Vila, his ministers and his representatives throughout the islands'. At this point, Mr Ravutia, if still awake, might enquire how all the missionaries and priests from the dozens of Christian denominations represented in the islands, who also tell his people how to behave and what to believe, fit into this grand plan. Finally, Mr Ravutia, whose brain must be quite addled by this stage, might have the temerity to ask how his own beliefs and tribal system of authority were to be accommodated.

The general state of duplication and confusion was reflected in the languages. In addition to a profusion of tribal languages around the islands there were, of course, English and French, both of which were official languages, plus Bislama (also known as Bichelamar), a sort of pidgin Franglais. One of my favourite examples of the latter was the Bislama name for the national statistics office: 'offis long big numba'.

All this duplication did have some benefits. Would you have chosen to eat in a British restaurant or a French restaurant? No contest really. But there were some areas of sacrosanct separation, particularly in the social life of the two European communities, cricket and *pétanque* being prime examples. Goodness only knows what the Melanesian population made of these bizarre customs being played out before them; perhaps they thought they were a rather slow form of European tribal dancing.

Few people outside the Pacific region seem to have heard of the New Hebrides or Vanuatu, although the islands do have some traditions that have become quite famous. One in particular is the forerunner of modern bungee jumping. The Naghol ceremony is a ritual leap from a wooden tower, about 100ft high, by young men on Pentecost Island to ensure a good yam harvest. The jumpers tie lianas to their ankles and throw themselves headfirst off the top of the tower with the idea that they should come to rest with their hair brushing the ground. This is a severe test not only of their manhood but also of their mathematical ability, because a mistake in the calculations can result in the poor unfortunate becoming a human tunnelling machine. I have recommended this failsafe method of ensuring good harvests to my farming friends in north Hampshire, but have not had any takers so far.

Another quirky claim to fame is the existence of semi-religious cargo cults on the island of Tanna. The most famous of these is the John Frumm Society, supposedly named after a black American serviceman in the Second World War who promised to return to the islands with refrigerators and other consumer goods if the people became his followers. They did but he didn't. Another group reportedly worship Prince Philip. On a flying visit to Tanna I jokingly remarked that they were welcome to him, but I had to retract my comment quickly when my hosts seemed interested in starting negotiations on his transfer.

A further distinguishing feature of life in the New Hebrides at this time was the mode of dress for men. Now, if the truth be told, most Melanesians I met wore shorts and T-shirts, but in some of the more isolated parts of the islands the penis sheath or penis pouch was still in vogue. This rather unusual item of clothing consists of a thick belt around the waist attached to a sheath over the penis holding it in an upright position. This is worn in splendid isolation without any other clothing, although an optional hibiscus flower behind the ear can set off the ensemble very nicely. One of my favourite postcards on sale in Port-Vila showed a football team dressed in this manner, and I sent a couple of these to my parents and to Auntie Audrey and Uncle Cyril in Birmingham. I added the comment that this form of dress was a bit uncomfortable at first but was fine once you got used to it. I learnt later that the reaction amongst my relatives was to assume that I had 'gone native' and they imagined me turning up at Heathrow wearing this attire.

Ron and I spent four wonderful weeks in the New Hebrides. We started off with the inevitable round of meetings in Port-Vila. The place was absolutely dripping with Europeans – colonial staff, agricultural officers, policemen, lawyers, plantation owners and managers, businessmen, merchant seamen, teachers, missionaries and church workers, anthropologists, not to mention the tourists who swarmed like bees off the cruise liners before disappearing as quickly as they had arrived. French and British civil servants were everywhere; we didn't meet anyone of Melanesian origin for days.

These were the last years of the gravy train. Not only did the British civil servants receive their salaries but their children were educated at British public schools and flown out each holiday to the South Pacific. For those with several children the cost was astronomical, all borne by the Exchequer. This nonsense continued into the 1980s, with some British agriculturalists and other expatriates working in Africa and elsewhere expecting the aid programme to pay all such costs and sometimes specifically taking jobs in order to finance their children's education. When I argued that the aid budget would be better spent on educating Africans rather than the children of expatriates, they thought this was heresy.

Thankfully there was only one Department of Agriculture. The Chief Agricultural Officer was a Frenchman, Monsieur Deroses, and, of course, his deputy was a Brit. The main mission in life of Monsieur Deroses during our visit seemed to be to get us drunk, a task successfully accomplished on several occasions. I never discovered whether this was simple generosity or a desire to see Brits doing stupid things. A touching the toes contest without bending the knees, while singing the National Anthem, springs to mind but we declined his challenge to follow his example of eating snails picked up from the garden. Monsieur Deroses was very proud of his ability to drink vast quantities of beer without any apparent effect and Ron, conscious of the need to maintain national pride, was eager to match him. My efforts to decline further bottles were brushed aside with questions about my masculinity.

One evening, after one of Monsieur Deroses's impromptu soirees, I was driving us back to our hotel on the edge of town in our borrowed Mini Moke (an open-topped vehicle of unmatched British engineering prowess capable of 30 mph on a good day) when the brakes failed on the steep approach road. 'Weeeeeeeeeeeeeeeh!' said Ron, who seemed not to have grasped the seriousness of the situation. Although I had consumed several Kronenbourgs fewer than him, I was still way past any sensible breathalyser limits, if such things had existed in the New Hebrides, but I was conscious that we were about to break the land speed record for a Mini Moke before embarking on a water speed record in the Pacific Ocean if we failed to stop before reaching the approaching shoreline. A combination of grinding gear changes, handbrake application and aiming at a grassy bank brought us to a halt, resting, appropriately enough, against a coconut palm. A smell of petrol and burning rubber pervaded the air, blotting out the usual tropical fragrances. Ron's automatic reaction, a few seconds after the Moke came to rest, was to reach for his cigarettes and matches, until I gently pointed out that he was in danger of blowing us up. 'I need a beer,' said Ron.

Fortunately, our main contact for assisting us with the feasibility study was the British Deputy Chief Agricultural Officer. His first task was to take us to a briefing meeting with five representatives of the British National Service Finance Branch who were supposed to monitor our progress during our stay. To illustrate the chaotic state of the colonial regime at the time, this office was abolished the following day on instructions from London. I think that our visit and their demise were unconnected, but it was a little unnerving.

Putting this bureaucratic nonsense aside as quickly as possible, we started the real work. We had a wonderful excuse for travelling around the main islands because we needed to decide which of them would make the best location for a desiccated coconut factory. Nut supply was a big issue because we calculated that the proposed factory would need about 30 million nuts per year and you do not source such a large number from wild palms growing along the seashore. We spent a great deal of time bouncing around on potholed tracks visiting coconut plantations, smallholder plots and research stations (like any other crop, there is a complicated agronomy associated with commercial coconut growing). Most of the existing nuts were used for copra production, which was the major export of the islands, but desiccated coconut would potentially yield a much higher income from the same number of nuts.

Travel between the islands was by small plane because the distances were too great for boat trips to be feasible in the time available. Air Melanesie was equipped with a fleet of Britten-Norman Islanders and Trilanders, nine and fifteen-seater planes, for which you had to be weighed as well as your luggage, prior to embarkation, so that the correct weight distribution and seating arrangement could be worked out. Admittedly appearances might have been deceptive, but the pilots all seemed to fall into two groups, either 20-year-old Australians or Gauloises-smoking Frenchmen in their seventies.

My white knuckles were in evidence for much of the time during these flights, particularly during the frequent tropical storms that made these flimsy metal tubes behave like the paper planes I used to make at school that would never fly in the direction intended. The grass landing strips on some of the islands resembled the North Downs, and one of them had a cemetery conveniently placed at the end of a bumpy runway that had more than once been brought into service directly from the crash scene a few feet away. When in the air it was always a great relief to see the vague outline of land appearing on the horizon, because there is something very disconcerting about flying low over an endless and empty ocean with no land in sight and the certain knowledge that the sea below is heavily populated with some very large and very welcoming sharks.

We quickly decided that the best location for the factory would be the largest island of the group, Espiritu Santo in the north, the scene of a lot of Second World War activity as featured in James A. Michener's *Tales of the South Pacific*. Among the legacy items left by the Americans were a lot of Nissen huts, some very serviceable coral roads and a number of individuals in their mid-thirties with rather paler skins than their fellow citizens. As well as the largest supply of nuts, the island also boasted a good deep-sea port for the export of the finished product at Luganville, universally known as Santo, the main town.

We based ourselves in Santo and set about carrying out the fieldwork for our project. As always this was the most fascinating part of the trip because it brought us into direct contact with a cross-section of the disparate groups of people living on the island, ranging from the Melanesian population to the European plantation owners to the Chinese traders (who might supply the building materials for a factory) to the Indian shipping clerks (who would organise the onward transport to overseas markets). The indigenous population in the rural areas mostly lived in simple huts surrounded by their easily grown staple foods – root crops such as yams and taro, fruit trees and the ubiquitous coconut palms, some planted into smallholder plantations by the more industrious villagers. Pigs supplied both meat and status, particularly in the form of the curved tusks that were so carefully nurtured by their owners. Cheek by jowl with these traditional scenes, which would not have changed greatly over many generations, were the plantations and copra driers owned by Europeans, mostly French.

When we learned that one of the plantation managers we would meet the following day did not speak any English, Ron assured me that an interpreter would not be necessary. He was very proud of the fact that he had recently delivered a paper in French to a scientific conference in France attended by oilseeds specialists from many countries. Only later did he admit that, although he had read the paper in French, it had actually been translated by a fluent French speaker and in the question session afterwards he had barely understood any of the points that were raised. But, confident that I was in the company of a linguist who would put my own 'O' level French to shame, I agreed that we could dispense with translation assistance. I should have known better, particularly as the meeting was in the afternoon after a full French lunch, including wine, as the guest of one of the French agricultural officers.

Ron started off the meeting quite well with a carefully rehearsed explanation of our purpose and an anecdote about his recent triumph in the conference hall. The manager looked suitably impressed and launched into a discourse on plantation management including the frequent problem of hurricanes putting right angle bends in his nice straight palms. Up to this point Ron had performed quite well, but he had now run out of pre-prepared questions and was beginning to yawn rather frequently. With a cheeky grin he said, 'Stephen veut poser un question'. This shook me out of my stupor and I stammered out an idiot question about why the coconuts in the New Hebrides were so much smaller than the nuts in the Philippines. A long-winded and highly technical answer followed, of which I did not understand a word. Ron also looked baffled but, worse still, he was losing the battle to stay awake and was ebbing into slumber. The whole scene was reminiscent of Eddie's siesta in Kabul.

In a moment of insight amidst the alarm that this situation

engendered, I realised that the advantage in both cases was that each person had ceased his unpleasant habit. There was a lapse in Eddie's nose picking, and even Ron could not smoke when asleep. I looked at him out of the corner of my eye and realised that with his head forward and his hands on his notepad below the height of the large wooden desk that separated us from the manager, he probably appeared to be taking copious notes. Anyway, the manager seemed not to have noticed and I let him plough on with his explanation with an occasional, 'C'est vrai' or 'Zut alors' thrown in at intervals, probably entirely inappropriately, to show that at least I was awake.

My state of panic heightened when it became obvious from the manager's body language that he had embarked upon telling a joke. I made an enormous effort to translate some of the words so that I could laugh at the appropriate moment. The joke seemed to have something to do with the benefits of combining cattle farming and coconut production so that when the nuts fell from the trees they would become impaled on the horns of the cattle, thus dehusking the nuts ready for transportation to the desiccated coconut factory. As the joke progressed I formed my face into a smile and inwardly debated whether a full-scale guffaw or a medium chortle would be more suitable. At what seemed to be the appropriate moment I let rip with a guffaw, which seemed to please the manager and also had the desired effect of shaking Ron out of his forty winks. Realising that laughter seemed to fit the moment, Ron joined in gamely before lighting a cigarette. He later claimed that he had only been asleep for part of the time, twenty winks perhaps, and to prove this he pulled my leg for years afterwards whenever we met at institute functions by whispering in my ear, 'C'est vrai, Stephen, c'est vrai'.

The invitation I had been dreading arrived the next day. It was from an English agricultural officer who kindly invited us to join his family the following Sunday on a speedboat trip to some nearby uninhabited islands where there were glorious palm-fringed beaches leading down to a lagoon where the ocean was so clear that it was perfect for snorkelling over magnificent coral reefs. Optional water-skiing in the afternoon would follow a lunchtime barbecue. My heart sank. The knowledge that family and friends at home would kill for such an opportunity only made the situation worse. Now was the time to make my humiliating admission: 'I can't swim'. I might also have added, 'I don't like sun-bathing and I avoid boats smaller than the QE2', but resisted this temptation on the basis that I already sounded like a total wimp and did not want to come over as a complete miseryguts as well.

I made a mental note to request the institute only to send me to landlocked countries in future so that I could avoid having to make the confession that I swim like a brick. On land I am quite a fit and athletic person, so I regularly face an interrogation about my lack of aquatic ability. This always stumps me. I usually mumble something about schools not teaching swimming when I was a lad and then sometimes go for the sympathy vote on the basis that I never had holidays as a child except in Derby, which is about as far removed as it is possible to be from a sun-drenched coastal resort with excellent water sports facilities.

Tired of having to offer such explanations, a few years later I did enrol for an adult learners' class at Isleworth Baths in London together with six old ladies, who were only there for the conversation, and a West Indian guy called Julius, who soon became known as the human torpedo because he could swim the crawl under water but could not replicate this feat on the surface. I went along to these classes a couple of times and had progressed to the level of swimming half a width, albeit with the assistance of armbands and a float, but seldom managed more as I was usually torpedoed and sunk by Julius. Further help was offered by the youths who took up position in the seating area next to the pool with shouts of 'spastic!' and other words of encouragement. Another overseas trip foreshortened my attendance at this course and somehow I never did find the enthusiasm to go back.

In the event I really did enjoy our day on the tropical island paradise. I politely declined the invitation to water-ski but, under Ron's tutelage, I did engage in a little gentle snorkelling (in about two feet of water).

All this was good fun, but the greatest pleasure for me during our month-long stay came from the 'bush' trips out to plantations and villages on the various islands. The people were universally friendly and mostly lived in highly picturesque villages set on the shoreline against a backdrop of volcanoes and densely forested hillsides. They had very few material possessions but also appeared to have no great desire for them. All the food they needed grew without much effort and they seemed happy.

This idyllic picture gives a hint of the main reason why a desiccated coconut factory would have been a high-risk venture in the New Hebrides. After our exhaustive investigation of all the factors that feed into a feasibility study, Ron and I had severe reservations about labour availability and reliability. We satisfied ourselves that most other factors were in place. A good potential market existed for the product, a suitable site for the factory had been found, enough coconuts could have been procured, adequate shipping connections existed and so on. But the minimum economic size of a factory would have required about 300 workers (some factories in the Philippines employed more than 1,000 people), and would have been the largest factory employer in the islands at the time. We had in-depth discussions with a number of employers and discovered that it was quite common for workers to go AWOL for a month or more after growing tired of factory discipline, monotonous tasks and working regular shifts, six days per week. Who could blame them?

This is a recurrent dilemma in many parts of the developing world, not only in small island economies in the Pacific and the Caribbean but also in parts of Africa. If I wear my economist hat I can make a strong case for saying that any national economy needing to import oil, vehicles, machinery and other essentials, plus operate an education and health system, must direct its inhabitants into economically productive activities. You cannot have one without the other, not unless you happen to be sitting upon a sea of oil or a mountain of gold. But the economic argument falls flat when you are confronted with an individual whose idea of work is to wander over to the nearest tree and pick a pawpaw for tea.

We were not allowed to say that workers were unreliable or lazy but instead had to use the PC aid jargon of the day by saying that 'their leisure preference is high'. Well, the leisure preference of many New Hebrideans was off the scale. Perhaps a strategy for the national economy based on tourism, offshore banking, a tax haven and a flag of convenience would be more suitable for a population with an antipathy to factory work but such policies seldom generate sufficient wealth to provide for all the needs of the nation.

After completing our fieldwork, Ron and I bid a reluctant farewell to the New Hebrides and went our separate ways. My visit to the USA started off by arriving in Los Angeles ten minutes before I left Port-Vila, courtesy of the International Date Line. I had been on business trips to the USA before, but never to Los Angeles, so during the stopover en route to Chicago I jumped in a taxi at the airport and asked to be taken on a whistle stop tour of Hollywood, Sunset Strip, Mann's Chinese Theatre and the other main sights. Thus in the space of one day I ran the full gamut of contrasts that our world has to offer, from simple thatched huts to the massive mansions of the film stars in Beverly Hills, from penis pouches to the designer chic of Macy's and Bloomingdales and from potholed tracks to the Los Angeles expressways. All very interesting, but I was glad to leave; it was too big, noisy and suffocating. My next stop was worse.

The temperature in Chicago on 20th February 1978 was about 20 degrees below freezing. Snow was piled up against the ground floor windows of the buildings and a biting wind whistled in off Lake Michigan. I sat on the 96th floor of the Hancock Building looking down on this scene and regretted my decision not to carry a coat with me on my round-the-world trip. Moving on swiftly to New York, one of my favourite cities and enormously preferable to Los Angeles, I met smartly dressed and affluent traders who spent their entire working lives buying and selling desiccated coconut. A few more meetings with major food and confectionery companies and then home to London, where I spent the next week in bed with influenza.

What was the outcome of all this work? Well, hopefully the market report proved useful to many desiccated coconut producers and prospective producers around the world, but the factory was never built. Apart from the reservations that Ron and I expressed about the labour situation and the modest level of forecast profitability, there were other things going on that were likely to jeopardise any prospective projects at that time. The UK and France found it difficult to agree on anything to do with the condominium at the best of times, but with the independence of Vanuatu looming, their attention turned to more immediate political problems.

Another event acted as a further disincentive to any new investment on the island of Espiritu Santo. The NaGriamel separatist movement wanted independence for the island and the return of land to the indigenous people. In 1980, a few months before the official independence date for all of the New Hebrides, Jimmy Stevens led a coup and declared Espiritu Santo to be the independent state of Vermana. This is possibly the only coup ever led by a forklift truck driver. It was quickly put down, but not before briefly hitting the headlines around the world and frightening off any potential investors.

The lack of action on building a factory was understandable in the light of our findings and the confused political situation, but was deeply disappointing all the same. The purpose of a feasibility study is to examine all the pros and cons related to a proposed project, and it can be argued that a negative outcome is just as valuable as a positive one because it may save a great deal of time, money and effort being wasted on a white elephant venture. A feasibility study should never be a rubber-stamping exercise for a positive decision already made in advance, although I have been in the position where this was expected. It is easy to rationalise and justify the lack of action but, for me, it was yet another disappointment – I craved to see concrete results that would make a real difference to poor people's lives in developing countries, but it was obviously going to be much more difficult than I had expected.

I learnt that most aid missions, with notable exceptions, result in no action at all. The reports just gather dust on the shelves of ministries and aid agencies. Inaction and duplication seemed to be integral parts of the process. Some subjects have been studied so often by different aid agencies that you could wallpaper the walls of the ministries with the paper from the reports and still have lots left over. Bananas in the Windward Islands and horticulture in Kenya are two examples of subjects that have been massively over-studied by the aid community, including me.

In my early years as an 'expert', the slow realisation that most of the work resulted in no concrete action became a major source of frustration. Man months and man years of time were spent by experts assiduously collecting relevant information leading to conclusions and recommendations which were written up in reports, with presentations given of the findings to interested parties, and then nothing would happen. On occasion this was for perfectly valid reasons, such as the Russian invasion of Afghanistan putting an end to plans to implement our recommendations in the wheat sector. At other times it seemed as if the aid agencies and the recipient governments were just going through the motions of appearing to address problems while knowing little, if anything, of any real benefit would result.

I spoke about these frustrations with my immediate boss at the institute, who was a kindly chap, approaching retirement age, with a background in the colonial service as an agricultural officer. He told me that few of the aid studies he had been involved with over many years had ever had their recommendations implemented.

To anyone who really wanted to get things done and to make an impact in developing countries, this was depressing news. I stayed at the institute for six years and my own experience was similar. I was lucky enough to visit some fantastic places, but the positive contribution to development was much less than I hoped. Later, in 1983, when I switched employment to a private consultancy company, working on international projects for both private sector clients and aid agencies, the success rate for getting recommendations implemented improved, but not by enough to satisfy my expectations.

Zambia 1970, my garden on the Mungwi Secondary School site with 12-foot python skin. Thankfully, I never saw a live one

South Africa December 1969, 250 miles north of Pretoria, where my lift dropped me, as explained in the text.

The Victoria Falls Bridge, on the border of Rhodesia (now Zimbabwe) and Zambia, which I crossed on foot in January 1970, having heard (incorrect) news earlier in the day that the Rhodesian Security Forces had closed the border due to "insurgent activity". Another close shave. Aerial photo taken on a return trip in 2015.

Kenya 1970. Many Masai make holes in their earlobes for adornments and this gentleman had inserted an (empty) tin of Heinz spaghetti.

India 1971, no caption necessary!

Khyber Pass 1971, the PBK "hippy bus" still functioning at this point, although painfully slow on the steep gradients.

Iran 1971 - one of many mishaps with the bus, in freezing temperatures. A few days later the bus "died" for good.

Afghanistan 1977: the smaller Buddha of Bamiyan, standing 125 feet (38 metres), carved into the sandstone cliffs in the 6th century and blown up by the Taliban in March 2001.

Afghanistan 1977, the larger Buddha of Bamiyan, standing 180 feet (55 metres), with restoration work being attempted on this magnificent monument, over 1400 years old. It was all to no avail thanks to its total destruction by the Taliban.

Afghanistan 1977, the main road from Bamiyan to Mazar-i-Sharif through the Hindu Kush mountains.

Afghanistan 1977, the Kuchi encampment in Helmand province where
I nearly sat on grandma.

Nepal 1980, on the road in eastern Nepal visiting tea estates, with the Himalayas in the
background

Nepal 1980, a typical trail scene, many miles from the nearest road. Notice the sick lady being carried by "ambulance", sitting in a doko and being carried over mountainous paths by a strong man.

Nepal 1980: an ex-Gurkha member of a survey team I supervised in eastern Nepal carrying out research on the marketing of agricultural products in village markets. Typical magnificent hill scenery in the background.

New Hebrides (now Vanuatu) 1978, market ladies selling their produce in leisurely style in Port Vila, the capital.

New Hebrides (now Vanuatu) 1978. I am visiting yet another coconut plantation on the island of Espiritu Santo, sustained by drinking the cooling water of a freshly harvested coconut.

New Hebrides (now Vanuatu) 1978, having just landed on the undulating grass runway at the "airport" on the island of Tanna in a typical Air Melanesie aircraft.

Sierra Leone 1979: a village palm oil pit, a far cry from the industrial-scale processing of the refined product in countries such as Malaysia.

Sierra Leone 1979. This gentleman insisted that I should not get my feet wet while visiting a palm oil mill in his village.

Sierra Leone 1979: children are expected to earn their keep at a young age.

Sierra Leone 1979. The paramount chief is wearing his preferred cowboy attire while his wooden "self" is dressed in traditional robes.

Nigeria 1989, village level production and sorting of ginger.

Chile 1985: local workers in a poultry slaughterhouse are required to recite the correct Arabic words while cutting the throats of chickens destined for export to the Middle East.

Chile 1985, a chick sexer at work.

Japan 1985, trade mission members visiting a poultry processing plant. There was considerable Japanese embarrassment on finding that none of their white boots fitted my big feet, thus necessitating plastic bags as an alternative.

Pakistan 1989, the potato section of a large wholesale market. Not a woman in sight.

Pakistan 1989, the watermelon section of a large wholesale market.

Pakistan 1989, members of the project team in front of a large estate owner's house.

Russian splendour 1991: Assumption Cathedral in the grounds of the Kremlin in Moscow.

Russian plumbing 1991, the first bathroom I saw on my first visit, at Kamenka sanitorium.

Russian winter 1991: "peasant" houses on a large state farm with horse-drawn transport.

Russian summer 1992, a beach scene – not on the coast but on the banks of Europe's longest river, the Volga, at Samara.

Russia 1991, a newly privatised shop, part of the first wave of mass retail privatisations across the whole country.

Russia 1993, a market in Togliatti ("home of the Lada") on the banks of the Volga, one of many babushkas trying to earn a few roubles by selling items from home to supplement meagre pensions.

Thirty-five years later, the Nigerian "deckchair" still has pride of place in my study and is a favourite with my grandchildren.

CHAPTER 8

SIERRA LEONE, 1979 AND 1986

My favourite greeting in all the world, so much more resonant than 'good morning', is 'How di body?' to which one answers, 'Di body fine'. This may well be followed by, 'How di day?' to which, of course, one replies, 'Di day fine'. This sequence may be repeated time and again with different subjects each time. 'How di wife (or wives)?' 'Di wife/wives fine'. 'How di goat?' 'Di goat fine' and so on.

The language is Krio and it is spoken in the Freetown area of Sierra Leone in West Africa. This is where the British deposited returned slaves in the late 18th and early 19th centuries, in the same manner as the Americans sent returned slaves to neighbouring Liberia. Hence the name Freetown and also the existence of nearby villages with such incongruous names as York, Kent and Waterloo. Although Krio is a form of Pidgin English, don't expect to go to Freetown and easily understand the conversations going on around you. As in Jamaica, Vanuatu and many other places, the local language has gone its own way to the extent that it is almost incomprehensible to a resident of the Home Counties if spoken at normal speed. However, if they slow down a bit and throw in some English learnt at school, then communication becomes easy.

It is almost impossible to use the Krio greeting without an accompanying smile. The two go together, hand in glove. I once hailed a taxi in Sydney, Australia, with a rather sullen-looking driver who fairly obviously originated from Africa. I asked him where he was from. 'You won't have heard of the place, it's called Sierra Leone'. 'How di body? ' I said. 'What?' he said, looking blank. I persevered, 'How di body?' His face broke into one of the biggest smiles I have ever seen as he replied, 'Di body fine'. Sullenness gave way to friendly, animated conversation. It made his day, and mine too.

'How di body' also seemed to be a particularly appropriate greeting to the prostitutes in the Paramount Hotel, the only hotel of any size in downtown Freetown. There were some much more luxurious hotels at Lumley Beach, a few miles out of town, on a particularly beautiful part of the peninsula where stuttering efforts were being made to breathe life into the embryonic tourist industry, but these were beyond our budget. So we stayed with the prostitutes at the Paramount. Not literally *with* them, but they were always present in the reception and bar areas in great numbers with lots of laughing and shrieking going on all the time. In the pre-AIDS awareness days of 1979 this seemed quite normal. Unlike the surreptitious approaches of prostitutes in Western hotels, in many parts of Africa the girls plied their trade in an entirely open manner with no apparent stigma attached.

I became particularly friendly with one of the prostitutes,

whom I nicknamed 'Flat hat' because of the little beret that she always wore. After a hard day's work in the hot and very humid conditions of Freetown I would return to the Paramount desperate for a beer. 'Flat hat' would often join me for a chat in the bar and we might watch a bit of television together. 'The Beverley Hillbillies' was her favourite programme. She established very early on in our relationship that I offered no business potential for her or her colleagues, but she loved to chat about different places in the world that she had seen on television.

The Paramount Hotel symbolises the downward path for Sierra Leone. In 1979 it was far from being a good hotel, judged by the standards prevailing in most of the rest of the world, but it was quite comfortable, provided edible food and, most amazing of all, had air-conditioning that worked. By the time of my next visit, in 1986, the prostitutes were still there, but almost nothing else was working. Both the electricity supply and the water supply were subject to prolonged interruptions, sometimes for days on end. Air-conditioning and hot meals became distant memories. The television had gone because there was no longer a functioning television station in the country. The mantra in all cases was 'shortage of spare parts' to explain why nothing worked. Even the radio station, which had sent a reporter to interview me in the Paramount Hotel in 1979, had closed down.

Another hotel in decline was the City Hotel in Freetown, supposedly the inspiration for the Bedford Hotel in Graham Greene's *The Heart of the Matter* where British colonial characters ordered gin-and-bitters from subservient bearers. Greene spent some of the war years working for the Foreign Office in Sierra Leone and the experience gave him the material for the novel, which was published in 1948. Less than four decades later the

City Hotel was a dilapidated bar and brothel where the main highlight of the week was an acrobat who entertained the crowd in the bar every Saturday lunchtime.

My visit to Sierra Leone in 1979 was my first time in West Africa. I had already developed a fascination for Africa originating from my time in Zambia, and I was keen to explore a new part of the continent. Inevitably I made comparisons. Mostly these were unfavourable. The climate was wet and very sticky. Some of the coastal scenery around Freetown, including the original 'lion mountain', which gave the country its name, was sensational, but there was nothing to rival the Rift Valley and high mountains of East Africa. There were no game parks to speak of. The standard of living of the people appeared to be much lower, which seemed inexplicable on the basis of the resources of the country, and most of the towns, including Freetown, were shabby even by African standards. The saving grace was the people. I wrote to my wife in October 1979 saying that the people I met were universally friendly, smiling and helpful. This applied equally to the Krio people (Creoles) in the Western Area and to the Temne, Mende and other tribal peoples around the provinces.

I would have been shocked and deeply dismayed if I had been told that 1979 represented a relative high point in the history of post-colonial Sierra Leone; independent since 1961. At the time it seemed like a low point, both economically and politically. The leader was President Siaka Stevens, a political tyrant who mismanaged the economy and the country for most of the period from 1967 to 1985. In a continent that has produced Bokassa, Amin, Mobuto and various other mass-murdering dictators, the best that can be said of Stevens was that he was not in their league, but he was a bad leader, widely believed to be amassing a fortune in ill-gotten gains. Accusations were made that he was pocketing large sums of money 'donated' by the local business community, made up of the so-called 'Lebanese' businessmen (actually most of them were of mixed race) and the ubiquitous Asian (mostly Indian) businessmen found in most parts of Africa.

A lot of the work carried out by 'experts' under the banner of international aid and development is a well-intentioned, yet misguided, waste of time and money. With the benefit of hindsight, this description probably applies to my visit to Sierra Leone in 1979. We were another Tropical Products Institute 'dream team' composed of a scientist and an economist. The scientist in this case was Dr David Dendy, head of the institute's cereal technology section, who had two great passions in his life, composite flour (see below) and madrigals. His prolonged efforts to interest me in the latter fell on entirely deaf ears, but he did stimulate my enthusiasm for the former, at least for the duration of our visit.

The idea of composite flour is to make bread from wheat flour that has been diluted with cheaper alternative raw materials such as maize flour or cassava flour. Some of the resulting breads are quite edible, while others are one level below dog biscuits. In a period of very high wheat prices composite flour makes good economic sense, because many developing countries like Sierra Leone cannot produce wheat and therefore must spend scarce foreign exchange on importing their requirements. Substituting some wheat with locally produced alternatives would not only save desperately needed dollars but also benefit local agriculture. So far so good. On the negative side, the quality of the bread suffers as the percentage of non-wheat products increases and, in the case of Sierra Leone in 1979, it was almost impossible to find commercially available quantities of alternative products. But the real killer blow to composite flour has been that wheat prices remained low for the greater part of the last three decades of the twentieth century and the early years of the twenty-first, thus severely reducing the attractiveness of finding substitutes.

Not being armed in 1979 with this foreknowledge about world wheat prices, I became fired up with enthusiasm for composite flour. This was encouraged by David's infectious zeal and by the fact that our institute had been commissioned to carry out this work by the Food and Agriculture Organisation (FAO) of the United Nations. Around the institute there was a certain extra cachet in carrying out assignments for the big multilateral aid agencies, instead of the usual British aid funding, and this was my first experience of working for FAO. Added interest was generated by the fact that we were to make a briefing visit to FAO headquarters in Rome on our way to Freetown.

Prior to our departure for Rome there was one big issue to resolve. The institute's hierarchy got their collective knickers in a twist over the question of who should be the team leader for our assignment. The terms of reference for the identification mission, as it was called in aid jargon, sent to the institute by FAO, specified that the marketing economist should be the team leader and the cereals technologist should work under his supervision. This presented a problem in that David was not only a fair bit older than me, but, much more significant in civil service terms, he was one rank higher. What a quandary!

It was unthinkable that FAO should be asked to make the cereals technologist the team leader because it was clear that this was not their preference. It was also unthinkable that the British civil service pecking order should be violated. It was a matter of supreme unimportance to me, but that was not the issue. An officially acceptable solution had to be found. After various senior level deliberations the stalemate was finally resolved. I was told in hushed and revered tones that a note was to be placed on the file. Wow! Big deal. This note said that although Jones was the team leader in the eyes of FAO, it was officially recognised that Dendy was the 'senior man'. This clarified absolutely nothing, in fact it made the situation more muddled, but all the top brass of the institute seemed very pleased with this compromise.

Rome was fascinating and fun. Our brief visit started off with a frenetic taxi ride. The driver explained that he ignored most red lights but, as a sop to the police, he stopped occasionally. This created a dangerous situation, however, because it took other motorists by surprise. Therefore, in the interests of safety, he was thinking of not stopping at any red lights in the future. We were deposited at the vast FAO building at Caracalla and were immediately accosted by a group of gypsy children in the car park. David's subsequent discovery that he had lost his money and travellers' cheques seemed not unrelated.

We were booked into the nearby Lancelot Hotel, run by the wonderfully named Mrs Music, in the aptly named Via Capo D'Africa, not far from the Coliseum. This turned out to be a very modest little hotel, not much more than a hostel, but within the very tight budget that FAO allowed us for food and lodging.

First impressions of FAO, with its excellent location and lovely roof terrace views over Rome, were that it was a glamorous place (certainly compared to my office in London's Clerkenwell Road) populated by an intriguing mix of clever people drawn from dozens of nationalities. Over the years, as I became familiar with the World Bank and other international aid organisations, I came to realise that FAO was a poor relation amongst the multilateral agencies, always strapped for cash, often because the USA had not paid its dues. Although FAO has been effective in certain areas of its work, it has always struck me as a largely ineffective body, mired in bureaucracy and diplomatic wrangling, never fulfilling its potential, as suggested by its name, of being the leading food and agricultural organisation in the world. But never mind, in 1979, as we were briefed by FAO officials who were almost as messianic about composite flour as David, the mix of the city of Rome and a global organisation striving to make great strides forward in agricultural development was quite intoxicating.

We flew to Freetown via Accra in Ghana, where we had an unscheduled six-hour wait. Paying dash or bribes really sticks in my gullet and I usually go to some lengths to avoid making this particular form of international aid disbursement. Just acting dumb quite often works, 'I'm sorry, but I really don't understand why I should contribute to the food bill for your 14 children', or playing the snotty Englishman, 'My good man, I refuse to pay bribes on principle and I demand to speak to your superior officer'. But none of this worked in Accra. I ended up paying a bribe to the immigration officer to get into the country, otherwise I would have spent six hours waiting on the tarmac, and, to add insult to injury, I had to pay a bribe to get out of the country, otherwise I would have missed the plane. None of my usual routines had any effect at all. I was an amateur in the midst of professionals.

We stayed in Sierra Leone for three weeks, having meetings with ministers, officials, and international aid workers. Just to make a change from the usual practice of aid missions, we also visited bakeries in Freetown and some of the other population centres to gauge their reaction to a potential new approach to bread-making. Compared to visits in later years, the fieldwork went very smoothly. The local FAO representative provided us with support and even held a couple of dinner parties in our honour. These provided a welcome relief from David's continuing suppertime efforts to interest me in the subject of madrigal singing in south Oxfordshire, but it also exposed us to contact with some of the European Neanderthals who were still to be found lurking around the African aid scene at this time. One particular couple, with a kind of 'White Rhodesia' mentality, were so unpleasant, racist and condemnatory of anything and everything local that I eventually asked them why on earth they were in Freetown. The answer, of course, was that they were earning a higher salary than they could get elsewhere.

Aid professionals have changed quite considerably over the course of my career. In the 1970s there were still many people whose careers had begun in colonial times. Many of these were hard working and sympathetic individuals with no racist tendencies, although they might still hanker after the old days of bearers and tiffin. However, others from this era were far more cynical about everything in the post-independence era and were more likely to have racist leanings. Then came my generation, who started their careers in the post-independence period. We were in between the old colonials and the bright new pins who entered the scene in more recent years. The latter are more admirable in many ways, being drawn from a far wider cross-section of countries, having higher academic qualifications and with few racist tendencies, but they can also be a bit boring and unimaginative. They seldom look up from their screens and tend to subscribe to the latest 'aid industry' theories and jargon in an unthinking way.

Words like gender, holistic, sustainable, paradigm, all of which have their place, are very in vogue and over-used. Other words, like agriculture, are out of favour and have been subsumed into concepts such as sustainable livelihoods. The laptop-attached aid industry professional of today, particularly in the field of natural resource-based livelihoods (agriculture by any other name), is a very different animal from most of those who were around at the end of the 1970s.

After visiting a lot of bakeries and carrying out exhaustive research into the likely availability of alternative products such as maize and cassava, we realised what we must say in our report. To David's credit, he did not allow his enthusiasm for composite flour to colour his judgement about our recommendations. It was clear that Sierra Leone was not ready for such an experiment and we proposed that the issue should be examined again in a few years' time in the light of international wheat price movements and the future availability of alternative raw materials. We had done a professional job and turned down a proposal that would have resulted in a white elephant project. Again, for me, this was a case of calculating negative benefits rather than my preferred option of pushing forward with aid projects that would yield clear, positive benefits, but finding such projects was difficult, particularly in Africa.

The fun, and the headaches, really began in 1986. I visited Sierra Leone three times on three separate projects in that year. After a lot of efforts to oust him, Siaka Stevens finally 'retired' in 1985, leaving the country he had ruled for nearly 20 years in a terrible mess. There were some hopes that his successor, J.S. Momoh, would prove to be an improvement, but early signs were not encouraging.

By 1986 I had been an 'expert' for nearly 10 years and I was familiar with having to acquire in-depth knowledge, frequently and speedily, about a wide range of products from the wonderfully complicated and multifarious world of agriculture. Some of the products were even more obscure and bizarre than composite flour; ugli fruit from Jamaica, xanthophyll from Ecuador (a product fed to chickens to make egg yokes more yellow) and cassava starch from Thailand, are just a few examples from my CV. At other times it was necessary to become knowledgeable about some of the major commodities of world trade such as coffee and tea.

The commodity that occupied my time for much of 1986 was palm oil. As usual, my ignorance was total when I started. I vaguely knew that palm oil is made from the small red fruits that grow on oil palm trees and that you crush these so-called fresh fruit bunches to extract oil, but that was about it. As before, when I had immersed myself in desiccated coconut and other commodities, I now delved deep into the mysteries of the palm oil industry.

By this time I was employed by a private consultancy company, mostly working on projects commissioned by the major international aid agencies. One of the smaller of these agencies was the Commonwealth Secretariat, based in London, which administered the development fund sourced from wealthier Commonwealth states that was spent on projects in the poorer member countries. The Com Sec, as it was usually known, was a bit-player in the aid world but it was also one of the main clients of my company at that particular time.

A few years earlier one of my colleagues had carried out a study commissioned by the Com Sec to assess the export opportunities for palm oil from Sierra Leone in neighbouring countries. Even by the standards of the aid sector this was a particularly stupid waste of money, because Sierra Leone had a substantial shortage of palm oil at that time and any fool knows that you don't start exporting a product when there is a considerable deficit in your own domestic market, particularly when that product is one of the main staples in the diet. Palm oil is the main cooking oil in the country and is widely used in stews and other popular dishes. In fact, exporting palm oil would probably have led to riots, because the price in local markets would have gone sky high.

To the Com Sec's credit they did pick up on the main message in the report that the palm oil industry in Sierra Leone was in such a state of disarray that a full analysis of the problem areas was needed, leading to an action plan for the revitalisation of the sector. Even better, the Com Sec selected my company to carry out this work. So it was that I arrived in Freetown in March 1986 as the team leader of a three-man mission to draw up a plan for the rehabilitation of the palm oil industry ranging from the large estates with their attached high-tech, but badly neglected, processing mills to the low-tech village level processors who either collected wild palm fruit or cultivated their own small plots.

My fellow team members consisted of a young and enthusiastic oil palm agriculturalist named Simon and an older, seen-it-it-all-before processing specialist called Bill. Both of them were highly competent technical specialists with a great knowledge of palm oil, whereas I knew next to nothing, at least when we started. My responsibility was for the economic and marketing aspects of the study as well as being the team leader. The rationale for this was that I could take the overview, embracing all the different disciplines involved. Technical specialists are renowned for having great expertise within a narrow area but are often not able to see beyond the end of their noses when it comes to appreciating the broader context. Bill was a classic example of this. He could tell you anything and everything about the engineering aspects of the mills, but the mental shutters came down when it was necessary to understand how agronomy or marketing impacted on his domain.

The joke about Simon was that he was in love with oil palm trees. As we travelled around large parts of the country he would yell for the Land Rover to stop so that he could disappear into the plantations or wild palms, where he could be seen climbing over them, caressing them and gazing dreamily into their fresh fruit bunches. He was a delightful enthusiast and I have seldom seen a person who loved his work more, which makes it all the more poignant that he decided to give it all up and take an IT job in the City of London only about one year later.

The trouble for Simon and others like him was that he arrived on the scene about two decades too late. In days gone by it was taken for granted that tropical agriculturalists, specialising in products like tea, coffee, cocoa and palm oil, would very often be British. From the toffee-nosed tea planters in 'Indjah' to the unsung heroes in the backwoods agricultural stations around the tropical world, the Brits were heavily represented. But they were a dying breed. By the latter years of the twentieth century the majority of tropical commodity specialists were Indian or Malaysian or Brazilian or from some other place where the product in question actually grew. Quite right too, but it was sad for the Simon generation that the opportunities gradually disappeared. The realities of providing for his wife and small children required that he bite the bullet, forsake his beloved oil palms and take an office job in the City. But at least in 1986 he could still indulge his passion.

Our visit to Sierra Leone in March 1986 got off to a bad start. It is the very nature of aid sector work in developing countries that team mobilisation and subsequent logistical issues give plenty of headaches, but this was an all-time bad experience. So-called 'long termers' i.e. those people on aid contracts of six months or more, tend to look down their noses at 'short-termers' (people like me) who just stay in a country for a few weeks and appear to behave like headless chickens, rushing around trying to collect all the necessary information and meet the relevant people in the short time allocated by the client organisation. Any significant delay usually throws these short-term missions into a spin but we (the short-termers) don't set the schedules or budgets, we just try to do a good job within the constraints.

It is very frustrating when you just want to get on with the job in hand but a series of calamities conspires to upset your efforts. Our visit started badly on 6th March 1986 when KLM managed to miss our connection in Amsterdam and then, after many hours of delay, returned us to London. Instead of reacquainting myself with the delights of the Paramount I spent the night in a hotel at Gatwick. We had better luck the next day and reached Freetown, only to find the city in darkness. Not only was there no fuel for the power station but, even worse, we were informed that petrol or diesel for vehicles was well-nigh unobtainable, even for our counterpart agency, the Ministry of Trade and Industry. Sierra Leone's credit was exhausted and the economic situation was so dire that the President himself was said to be running around the world trying to do deals, almost certainly shady ones involving diamonds, to get a tanker to be sent to the country before there were serious outbreaks of violence. Cars were parked at petrol stations for days on end and the situation in areas distant from Freetown was even worse.

Lack of a vehicle with fuel meant that we faced the prospect of carrying out a review of the palm oil sector without seeing any palms or processing facilities. The dreadful possibility arose of sitting in Freetown for three weeks, twiddling our thumbs, but then a gentleman named Ahmed appeared on the scene and saved our bacon. Although he was quite a high-ranking official in the Ministry of Trade and Industry, Ahmed had a sort of Del Boy persona combining great charm with a willingness to do dodgy deals that should not be questioned too closely. In spite of requests by the Com Sec in London, no preparations for our visit had been made, so Ahmed had to start from scratch in obtaining a four-wheel drive vehicle (the main roads were bad but the bush roads were impassable without 4WD), a driver and, most important of all, a 50-gallon drum full of fuel so that we could not only reach the oil palm growing areas but get back to Freetown again.

It took Ahmed a week to achieve these tasks. Most of the ministry's vehicles were laid up because of 'a shortage of spare parts'. The central bank had virtually no foreign exchange, so import licences for any form of equipment or spare parts were virtually unobtainable. The same refrain would be heard time and again to explain why the machinery in the palm oil factories was lying idle or the TV station had closed down or a restaurant was cooking outdoors rather than using its Western-style ovens.

Eventually Ahmed located a vehicle that we could use for one week and a driver who would take us, on condition that I was prepared to supplement his measly ministry wages and pay for his accommodation while away, both of which I was happy to do. Finding a 50-gallon drum took about a day, but filling it with petrol required another three days of wheeling and dealing.

While Ahmed was engaged in obtaining the necessary permits and then negotiating with all the parties involved, including the black marketers where necessary, we occupied our time by doing the rounds of the ministries and aid agencies. We were given the use of a small office in the Ministry of Trade and Industry, which must be the most depressing building I have seen in the world. The interior appeared to have been designed to encourage suicidal urges. It was dark and airless even when the electricity supply was working, but during blackouts the corridors gave one the impression of being down a crowded mine. Dark shapes emerged out of the gloom and the smell of body odour was overpowering.

Construction of the building had obviously never been completed and all the electric wires and cables just hung down from the ceilings and walls. The main protection against being electrocuted was that the electricity supply seldom worked. The lift hardly ever functioned, but most people took the wise precaution of avoiding it like the plague, preferring instead to run the risk of having their feet trodden on in the darkness of the overcrowded staircase. It was a great relief to emerge out of the front door of the building and take a breath of fresh air, but even then your troubles were not over because it was necessary to take evasive action to avoid the bat droppings which seemed to fall in bucketfulls from the nearby trees where these spooky beasts liked to hang out.

The air of melancholy was exacerbated by the ministry workers, who seemed to have little stomach for doing any work and spent their days reading newspapers, having a chat or just staring into space. In most Western countries idle office workers usually feel the need, at the very least, to look busy by putting up some pretence of activity. Such sensitivity does not exist in many parts of the developing world and it is not unusual to find people fast asleep at their desks. I made some vaguely critical remarks along these lines to Ahmed, who pointed out that I would probably not look very energetic if paid the pittance that they received, which in any case was three months late in being paid at that particular time. He had a point and I have to agree that on the occasions when I have directly recruited and paid workers in developing countries, in such roles as drivers, interpreters or survey staff, they have usually worked very conscientiously.

Unlike many of his colleagues, Ahmed was a hard worker and he laboured tirelessly in our cause, although I did find out later that he had an ulterior motive in that he was seeking employment with the Commonwealth Secretariat in London. In his position I would have done exactly the same thing, but it does highlight the dilemma that the best brains and the hardest workers in many of the poorest developing countries are often sucked out of the environment where they are needed most by joining the brain drain to the West. A job with the United Nations or some similar body is often the pinnacle of ambition for such people and who can blame them?

Eventually we were ready to set off on our tour of the major oil palm areas of the country. It had taken a week to make the preparations that would have taken a few hours in a Western country. We had barely started work on the main subject matter of our study but a third of the time had already elapsed. Most of the week had been spent achieving the seemingly simple task of getting a vehicle full of fuel on the road. Even now our troubles were not over. As we pulled away from the Paramount I noticed that we had no spare tyre. So much energy had been expended on getting fuel that another of the essentials had been forgotten. We spent the next two hours touring the dilapidated back streets of Freetown while Ahmed went from one place to another until we finally found a wheel that had a tyre with a tread that was slightly better than lethal.

En route to the town of Bo via Waterloo, we all felt exhilarated to have fled the city and escaped to the interior. We drank in the fresh air, so welcome after the stink of Freetown, except that, at regular intervals, the fresh air disappeared and the atmosphere became black as a result of villagers burning the bush scrub prior to cultivation. In many parts of Africa shifting cultivation is practised, whereby the people grow their crops on an area until the soil becomes exhausted before moving on to burn the scrub from another area in preparation for planting. Very often scattered wild oil palms would be eerily visible through the smoke and Simon would mutter sympathy for his friends as the flames lapped around the bases of their trunks. Usually the trees would survive this assault and the villagers would plant their maize, cassava or other crops around them and later harvest the oil palm fruit as part of the mixed farming system.

If there were world rankings for the palm oil industry, a country like Malaysia with its super-efficient plantations, factories and management, would be at the top of the table, followed by various other countries in South-east Asia and a couple in Africa. These countries supply palm oil by the tanker load to major international markets where the product has both edible (e.g. margarine) and industrial (e.g. soap) end uses. Somewhere near the bottom of the table would be Sierra Leone, with its dilapidated factories and neglected plantations.

In fact the most efficient part of the Sierra Leone industry was the village level processing based on local people procuring fruit from a variety of sources – wild palms, their own mini-plantations or pilfered from the government-owned estates – and then carried to pits where, in scenes slightly reminiscent of the treading of grapes in France in the traditional wine-making process, villagers would crush the fermented fruit prior to boiling. The resultant thick red gooey liquid was very different from the clear, refined oil of international trade, but the crude product sold like hot cakes in local markets, where great drums and buckets of the stuff were a regular feature.

If you wanted to find an example of public ownership of commercial activities in Africa resulting in chronic inefficiency, then look no further than the palm oil sector in Sierra Leone. There are many other candidates for the most corrupt and inefficient public enterprise in the continent, such as the commodity marketing board in Nigeria, whose skyscraper building mysteriously burnt down prior to a fraud investigation, but the Sierra Leone palm oil industry should be counted amongst them. One of the great mistakes in the first two decades of the post-independence era in Africa, encouraged by the aid agencies at the time, was the support given to government-owned commodity boards which became bastions of incompetence and were generally viewed by politicians and their cohorts as sources of easy pickings for lining their own pockets. The reluctance to engage with multinational companies, such as Unilever, or local business groups, sometimes owned by people of Asian origin, meant that these public sector monstrosities survived much longer than they should have done and did an enormous disservice to the cause of development for the ordinary people of Africa.

By the mid-1980s these lessons were being learnt and the move towards privatisation or partial privatisation was slowly getting into gear. So it was that the two largest oil palm plantations, with the two largest mills (neither of which were operational because of 'shortage of spare parts'), were in the process of being transferred to private ownership, but there were many other smaller government-owned plantations and mills that were in a shocking state of neglect. Both Simon and Bill, who had learnt their trade in countries higher up the palm oil league table, were deeply dismayed at the scenes that met our eyes on our tour round the country. The only rays of comfort, apart from village level processing, were two new small plantations and mills that had been established by local entrepreneurs. These were well maintained and offered some pointers and hopes for the future.

We rattled and bumped our way round about half the country, staying in government rest houses which were mostly very basic, until one night we stayed in a rest house that had once played host to Siaka Stevens and I found myself sleeping in a luxurious bed with a vast and elaborately carved headboard containing enormous numbers of electronic gadgets such as radios and multi-coloured lights, none of which worked.

It is not a comfortable climate for travelling, being hot and very sticky. Thankfully we were only at the start of the rainy season and in a few weeks' time regular downpours would ensure that the roads maintained their reputation for being mud baths to challenge even the most robust 4WD vehicles, particularly when the mud camouflages lurking boulders just waiting to tear off some vital part of the undercarriage.

Our vehicle was already heavy, what with five men and a 50-gallon drum, but our weight and overcrowdedness were added to at every village stop by people with heart-rending stories of why they needed lifts to the next town and the impossibility of finding any alternative form of transport. Ahmed was a soft touch in these matters, particularly when confronted by a lady with a touching tale, so we had plenty of company. In order to keep our spirits up, Ahmed kept us regularly supplied with palm wine, an alcoholic drink tapped from the oil palm, although I must admit I never developed a taste for this sickly liquid.

Disaster nearly befell us one day when we realised that the increasingly strong smell inside the vehicle was due to a tiny leak in our precious 50-gallon drum. We all had visions of being trapped in the bush for days, even weeks, until the national fuel shortage was alleviated – not a pleasant prospect. Thankfully the ever-resourceful Ahmed found a way of staunching the flow and we carried on our way, but rather more nervously than before.

Six months later the same team, but with one extra member, made another visit to Sierra Leone. In the intervening period our report, produced for the Government of Sierra Leone and funded by the Com Sec, was well received and in an unusual example of inter-agency cooperation the United Nations Industrial Development Organization (UNIDO), based in Vienna, funded a follow-up mission to prepare detailed plans for the rehabilitation and privatisation of the medium-sized government-operated plantations and mills. As part of this study it was necessary to visit several tribal chiefs, because their consent was needed for any change of ownership of the plantations located on their traditional tribal lands. Thus it was that I came to meet a collection of the most bizarre and colourful individuals I have met in Africa.

I was familiar with the term 'paramount chief' from my time in Zambia and knew that such people held dominion over very large areas and great numbers of people, albeit with much less real power than they had exercised in pre-colonial times. It was something of a shock to find that in Sierra Leone a paramount chief often had authority over a very modest area and a small number of people. Some of the chiefs lived in simple mud huts with thatched roofs, like their subjects, although others had corrugated iron roofs as a sign of their status. One lived in a modern house, built like an elongated bungalow with an extra room being added each time an extra wife joined the team.

The paramount chiefs varied greatly in their ages, level of education and general outlook on life. One, who was Western educated and had only one wife, was a director of the Bank of Sierra Leone. Another newly appointed chief had married four wives on the same day. Two of the chiefs were ladies, one of whom insisted upon being addressed as Madame Chief. The other female paramount chief was an old lady who received me in her hut sitting on a deckchair, which appeared to serve the purpose of a throne, wearing a piece of white cloth on her head, which seemed to correspond to a crown.

My favourite, and the most eccentric of the paramount chiefs, was a middle-aged gentleman who had adopted an unusual mode of dress. I was shown into a fairly simple hut and as my eyes adjusted to the darkness, I found myself confronted by a cowboy fully kitted out in Stetson hat, jeans and cowboy boots, like a character out of the film 'Blazing Saddles'. Totally gob-smacked and trying hard not to just stand there with my mouth open, I forced myself to concentrate on the job in hand and asked the chief if he would give his blessing to an aid project to privatise and rehabilitate the small plantation and mill located on his tribal lands. Like his fellow chiefs, he was fed up with government incompetence and very enthusiastic about any project that would generate much-needed income for his people. He expanded on these themes at some length but I fear my mind was wandering because, out of the corner of my eye, I became aware of a person sitting close to us with unnatural stillness. He didn't move a muscle for about fifteen minutes, and I realised that this was for a very good reason – he was made of wood. It was a life-size carving of the same chief in the full ceremonial robes of a paramount chief. He explained that he preferred to dress as a cowboy but his people expected him to dress as a chief, so he had had a wooden likeness made to pacify them. Later, I asked Ahmed if he could throw any light on the cowboy chief, but he just shrugged and said, 'He's a chief, he can do what he likes'.

Towards the end of our UNIDO-funded visit I was feeling pleased with the progress made and was confident that we could put forward proposals for a good project. As the team leader it fell to me to organise a celebratory meal for the team and our Sierra Leonean counterparts and their wives. I debated whether or not to invite a particular individual named Abdul, a fairly junior member of the Ministry of Trade and Industry, who had made only a minor contribution to our work. Feeling in a generous mood, I decided to invite him, and thus made one of my biggest gaffes in Africa. I usually prided myself on being sensitive to local cultures and aware of individual sensitivities, but in this case I got it badly wrong.

'You are the rudest man in the world,' said Abdul with real

venom. I was totally taken aback because all I had done was to invite him and his wife to join us for dinner at a restaurant. Abdul said that his wife had nothing to wear and I had light-heartedly replied that it did not matter if she came with nothing on. In a country where the standard female attire in many of the villages we had visited was a piece of cloth tied round the waist and nothing else, this comment might not have seemed out of place, but I had forgotten that Abdul was a Muslim from the Fullah tribe and I had insulted him greatly.

One of the team members, in an effort to defuse the situation, said that it was the sort of joke that we made in England and that he would not have been the least bit offended if I had made a remark about his own wife wearing no clothes. Although well intentioned this comment served only to confirm in Abdul's mind that the British were irredeemably corrupted and that he should sever all further contact with us. I could have kicked myself for being so stupid. I doubt that I would have made the same blunder in a country like Nigeria where the Islamic presence is much higher profile, but in Sierra Leone, with a lower percentage Muslim population, I had been thoughtless and verbally lax to the extent that I had given great offence.

Less than two months later I was back in Sierra Leone again, this time working on a lightning-quick ten-day contract for the World Bank. I'm not sure how they got my name but I received a call from Washington telling me that a combined World Bank and International Monetary Fund (IMF) team was going to the country to assess the possibility of organising a rescue package. The dire economic plight was clearly evident for all to see. The Leone, the local currency, had already been devalued by about 600% that year and agricultural labourers were receiving a wage of less than 50 US cents a day. The country was considered ripe for revolt (how right they were) and an IMF loan, with a World Bank structural adjustment package, was under consideration in an effort to avert economic and political disaster. They needed an agricultural marketing specialist to provide inputs to the team on issues relating to the pricing of major agricultural commodities such as rice.

In recent times the anti-globalisation movement has demonised the IMF and the World Bank as the bad guys in the 'aid industry', but in those days they were generally regarded as good guys. I was pleased to join their team, although I did believe that the economic medicine that was being prescribed was draconian. I agreed with the underlying structural adjustment ideas about removing subsidies and government interference in commercial activities, but I thought the timescale being envisaged for implementing the reforms was unrealistically short. I was overruled and the standard template was applied.

There was no question of staying in the Paramount Hotel on this occasion. The employees of the World Bank and the IMF were used to better things. For the first time in my various visits to Sierra Leone I stayed in one of the more luxurious hotels located at Lumley Beach. In the five-star hermetically sealed bubble of the Mammy Yoko Hotel, removed by some distance from the squalor of Freetown, there was a danger that you could lose sight of the realities of local life. In a similar vein, our transport from Lungi Airport to the hotel was by helicopter rather than the more arduous journey by road and ferry across the wide estuary of the Sierra Leone River. The battered old ferryboat, looking as if it had been sunk and refloated several times, staggered slowly backwards and forwards from bank to bank and the journey time from airport to town could often take quite a few hours. But the World Bank staff were in a permanent hurry and, unlike the other aid agencies, there never seemed to be any great shortage of money.

Working for three different multilateral aid agencies (the Commonwealth Secretariat, UNIDO and the World Bank) in the same country, in the same year, provided a study in contrasts. The poor relation was the Com Sec, which was always strapped for cash and could not afford the luxury of its own office in recipient countries. UNIDO occupied the middle ground, being a large organisation with substantial funds, and could just afford to maintain its own small office in Freetown, ably run by a very dignified Ethiopian gentleman. The World Bank was the deluxe organisation with seemingly very deep pockets and sumptuous offices in many countries.

Since then I have worked for the World Bank on a number of occasions and have always found the staff to be intelligent, well-qualified, motivated and hard-working. But they do tend to be over-prescriptive and to apply their set remedies in an arbitrary manner. In my opinion they do not deserve the opprobrium heaped upon them by the muddled anti-globalisation lobby, but they do have a tendency towards arrogance that can tarnish their image. An example from 1986 was the furore among World Bank employees when it was proposed that they should no longer be entitled to automatic first-class travel on all flights. They were up in arms at what they saw as an attack on their entirely justified perks. At a time when other aid workers, experts and all employed in the development 'industry' considered themselves lucky to travel in business class, and very often ended up in economy, this presumption of a right to luxury travel attracted a lot of criticism and strengthened accusations about remoteness from the people in recipient countries who the World Bank was supposed to be helping.

Pondering the fate of Sierra Leone from 1986 to today makes me sad and angry. 'Experts' are usually supposed to remain dispassionate about the poverty and suffering that exists around them. This is sensible advice, because we would quickly go mad if we became emotionally involved in all the hardship and iniquities that we witness, but I find detachment particularly hard in the case of Sierra Leone. Taking into account its diamond mines and other resources, it should be a rich little country with its small population of about 8 million people living in relative affluence, at least by African standards. Instead it is one of the most poverty-stricken places in the world, with a population traumatised by war and terror. Some of the worst atrocities perpetrated by one person against another in modern times have been carried out in Sierra Leone. Limbs have been cut off, eyes gouged out and children forced to kill their parents. The country where I remember walking around in both urban and rural areas in a friendly atmosphere, without feeling the least bit threatened, was transformed into one of the most dangerous places in the world, where the local population were subjected to some of the worst barbarity known to man.

From the late 1980s to 2000, successive leaders plundered the country. Occasional periods of stability were never long enough to get development programmes working effectively and most aid efforts, including those that I had been involved with, foundered in the general chaos. At intervals yet another tinpot warlord assembled an army of drug-fuelled children to try and establish himself as the chief plunderer, killing and maiming the population along the way. Power and greed for diamonds were the driving forces.

The West African disaster of the last two decades of the 20th century, which claimed up to half a million lives, primarily in Liberia, Sierra Leone and Côte D'Ivoire, has sometimes been called a Taylor-made disaster after Charles Taylor, the American-educated and Libyan-trained guerrilla leader. He destabilised and then ruled Liberia until forced into exile in the summer of 2003. He first came to prominence in 1989, and in 1991 he sent his henchman Foday Sankoh as head of the Revolutionary United Front (RUF) to capture the Sierra Leonean diamond mines. Thus the ten-year nightmare began. The best efforts of West African peacekeepers and the United Nations in the late 1990s proved to be largely fruitless, and it was not until the intervention of British troops in 2000 that stability was re-established.

Over the years, as I have watched the television images of mayhem in Sierra Leone, I have always wondered about the safety and whereabouts of two individuals, Dr Kobba and Bai Kamara. Dr Kobba is an amazing man who through willpower and the force of his considerable personality had built up a hospital in a remote area of Eastern Province close to the border with Liberia. In addition to being a medical doctor, whose training had included a long spell in Germany, he was also a successful entrepreneur in a country not noted for indigenous success in business activities. In order to fund the development and running of his hospital he had hit upon the idea of operating an oil palm plantation and mill. In 1986 he already had a plantation in excess of 1,000 acres and had plans to expand to more than 5,000 acres. According to Simon, the plantation was the best maintained in the whole country and Bill confirmed that the mill was in better condition than all similar installations. Not content with just selling palm oil, Dr Kobba, in true entrepreneurial style, had recognised the added value possibilities of installing a small soap-making factory, which was bringing in much-needed revenue for his precious clinic.

Dr Kobba used all means at his disposal to drive the dream forward. He inveigled medical volunteers from Germany and other countries to work on a voluntary basis in his hospital. Dutch aid funds had been secured to finance the expansion of the oil palm business. Other sources of funding were exploited with consummate skill and a lot of wheeler dealing. Like everyone else who came into his orbit I was treated to a tour of the simple, yet impressive, hospital and fell under his spell when asked to use my influence with aid agencies to help expand the agricultural businesses. Unfortunately the clinic's location at Mobai was quite literally in the firing line of the rebels who spilled over the border from Liberia, and the fruits of Dr Kobba's brave endeavours were destroyed. The details are sketchy, but I believe that the clinic was attacked in 1991 and that many people, including the doctor's staff and relatives, were killed or mutilated. Dr Kobba escaped through the forest and I heard from him some years later in Freetown but then lost contact.

Bai Kamara was a quieter and more unassuming character. I first met him in 1979 when he was assigned to David Dendy and myself as our counterpart officer. At that time he was a young graduate working in the Ministry of Agriculture and he was given the job of helping us to organise our programme, accompanying us to all our meetings in Freetown and elsewhere, assisting us to unearth statistics and other information and generally to contribute to the success of our mission. In other words he fulfilled the role in 1979 that Ahmed undertook in 1986. A good counterpart officer makes a world of difference on overseas trips, and I was very lucky in all my visits to Sierra Leone. I have occasionally been much less fortunate in other African countries, where I have sat around in hotel lobbies for hours on end waiting for a counterpart to arrive only to find that he was sleeping off the drinking excesses of the night before. Such experiences serve to reinforce the knowledge that making progress on short-term aid missions is heavily dependent upon the quality of the local support.

Bai carried out his duties in 1979 with competence and much good humour. He kept us sane when we got exasperated with the frustrations of African working life, like transport not turning up or people forgetting to attend meetings or the phones not working or a thousand and one other things. After I commented that I had been unable to find groundnut stew on any of the menus of the restaurants we had visited, he invited us back to the family home for an excellent meal. I was very pleased to repay his hospitality some years later when Bai stayed at my house in London for a weekend when he was attending a training course in Birmingham. I remember his endless patience with my two young children, who thought it very funny to repeat over and over again, 'Bye bye Bai'. He just smiled his enormous smile and played along with the game. In 1986 I visited Bai, his wife and children at their home in Freetown and we kept in touch by post for some years afterwards, but the communications stopped at the time of one of the worst outbreaks of violence and I have feared the worst ever since.

Sierra Leone is rich in resources. Diamonds ought to be its best friend, but they have actually been the poisoned chalice and are now known as 'blood diamonds'. The country has other mineral wealth and good agricultural potential. All this counts for nothing when civil society and the economy have been destroyed. No one would deny that the prime offenders were Charles Taylor (convicted of war crimes in the Hague in 2012), Foday Sankoh (who died of natural causes in 2003) and those Sierra Leoneans who were prepared to destroy the lives of their fellow citizens for their own selfish ends. As if all that was not enough, the country faced the Ebola crisis in 2014/15, but the greatest damage had already been done. Should not the outside world have taken effective action to stabilise the situation long before the British army arrived in 2000? Did not the ordinary, decent people of Sierra Leone deserve protection at an earlier date? It should not be left to the bilateral efforts of former colonial powers to intervene at the eleventh hour when destruction is already nearly complete. Such interventions, although clearly welcome in the Sierra Leone case, will always be open to accusations of neo-colonialism. Rather, there should be multilateral action with appropriate legal backing through the United Nations or African organisations. Easier said than done and the history of such multilateral interventions in Sierra Leone is not good, but this should stiffen the resolve to do it better by providing the appropriate resources and training. The girl with both her hands cut off should not live in fear that the same will happen to her children.

CHAPTER 9

NIGERIA, 1985 AND 1989

'There's been a coop, sah', said the man behind the desk in answer to my question. I was none the wiser. We were standing in the foyer of the Eko Holiday Inn on Victoria Island, Lagos, on 27th August 1985 and I wanted to know why I was being prevented from leaving the hotel. After much effort I had at last managed to arrange appointments that day with the Permanent Secretary of the Ministry of Agriculture and the Perm. Sec. of the Ministry of Commerce and Industry. For several days I had been told that these gentlemen were not 'on seat' but now, after using all the well-connected intermediaries I could find, I had tied them down. Knowing that the Lagos traffic would be as impenetrable as ever, I fretted that I would be late for these greatly prized meetings. The suit I was wearing intensified my discomfort. Why on earth did Nigerian politicians and senior civil servants wear dark three-piece woollen suits in this heat and expect their visitors to dress equally smartly? The only exceptions were those Nigerians who wore traditional robes, but visitors were still expected to dress as if they were going to a wedding.

What was the man behind the desk talking about? The only coop I could think of was a chicken coop. At last the penny dropped. 'Oh, you mean there's been a military coup'. 'Yes, there's been a coop, sah'. My heart sank. There was no time to go into the intricacies of the English language. 'Is there a curfew?' 'Yes, sah.' 'How long will it last?' 'No idea, sah'.

'Oh, dear' I said to myself, or words to that effect, as the possible consequences of the situation unfolded in my brain. The immediate, enormous frustration at having my business plans for that day disrupted gave way to broader questions of personal safety. Was there a bloody civil war going on? Was I in great personal danger? Would I ever see my wife and children again? My thoughts became more and more melodramatic. It occurred to me that my unfounded reputation among friends in London for being a British secret agent might be boosted by this experience.

I went outside to see if there were any signs of explosions or gunfire. Apart from the soldier by the main gate, who motioned me to go back into the building by twitching his rifle, there was no sign of anything different, just an eerie hush as a result of there being only a fraction of the usual cacophonous traffic noise.

As I walked up the four flights of stairs to my room I had time to reflect on the numerous horror stories I had heard about Nigeria and all the people who had said that I must be mad to go there. It was one of the least popular places to visit among people employed in the 'aid industry' and I knew several who refused point blank to go there. Lagos, in particular, was disliked at this time because of its reputation for crime, grime, expense (it often topped the most expensive city in the world league table) and the worst traffic jams on the planet. People competed with each other for the record of the longest time taken to get from the centre of town to the airport. Seven hours was one claim I had heard. This is the city that came up with the scheme that cars with licence plates ending in even numbers could use the roads on alternate days and cars with plates ending in odd numbers could drive on the other days.

Another reason for the country's unpopularity was that Nigerians had a reputation, even among their fellow Africans, for arrogance and rudeness. I remember being in a hotel restaurant in Lusaka in Zambia some years before when a customer was making rude and noisy complaints to the staff and demanding to see the manager. My Zambian friends all muttered under their breath that the man must be Nigerian. There were no special pointers to his nationality from his dress or accent, but they said that only a Nigerian would behave in that way. They said that oil wealth and being the most populous country in Africa combined to make Nigerians big-headed. It turned out that my friends' assumption was correct. In the interests of fairness I should say that I have met large numbers of Nigerians who do not deserve to be tarred with the same brush, but even they would probably acknowledge that their country, at least at this time, was not very popular with foreigners.

I switched on the television in my room and found that all programmes had been replaced with sombre martial music. Increasingly flustered, I turned to a higher authority – no, not God, but the BBC World Service. At this time, before television news channels like CNN became regularly available in hotel rooms, I was a great devotee of the radio broadcasts from Bush House. It had been a lifeline since I first travelled to distant lands in 1969, especially in times of stress, war and important football matches.

I thought that I could rely on the BBC to give me the low-down on what was really happening in Nigeria, if only I could get good reception. As ever, that was the problem. Over the years I have draped long lines of wire around rooms to act as aerials and hung out of windows, clutching my portable radio, until I was in danger of falling to the street below, just to hear the familiar music followed by the wonderful words, 'This is the BBC World Service, here is the news'. The wavelengths on short wave are etched in my memory – 15400, 12095, 9410, 6195 and many more. I have spent countless hours holding the radio to my ear, partly so that my body acted as an aerial and partly in an effort to disentangle the words from the damned interference that always reaches a crescendo just at the critical moment and obliterates the vital item of news you have been waiting for. I tried all these tricks and eventually managed to find good enough reception to be told that there were unconfirmed reports of a coup in Nigeria but no other information was available. Thanks very much.

Knowing that the television station was always one of the first places to be taken over in an African coup, I turned the set on again and after a few more minutes of martial music a soldier appeared, sitting at a desk in front of a Nigerian flag. I was later to learn that this rather fearsome looking individual, with deep tribal scarring across his face, was Sani Abacha, who would lead his own grab for supreme power many years later (in 1993) and become infamous as the tyrant who supposedly died of an excess of Viagra and related activities in 1998. In 1985 Abacha was one of the plotters, but not the leader. His job was to appeal for calm and say that everything was going to be better and a full broadcast to the nation would be made within a few hours.

None of this satisfied my thirst for knowledge about what was really going on. I tried using the phone, but the hotel operator said that all lines were dead. Looking out of the window was no help. There were no fireballs over Lagos or tracer bullets in the sky or any of the other things that always acted as a backdrop to Kate Adie when she was reporting on similar incidents around the world.

In search of more information I went downstairs and ran across two Belgian guys who I had spoken to on a few occasions the previous week. They had unpronounceable names, so I had christened them, in my own mind, Bill and Ben. They were engaged in some sort of business in the country and had lived permanently in the hotel for a number of years. When asked about their bizarre choice of living arrangement they explained that an apartment in town, although cheaper, would be a target for burglars, particularly during the long periods when they were at home on leave. No matter how bad the security situation, the idea of living in a hotel room for even a couple of months, let alone a number of years, would have driven me up the wall, but they appeared to be very content. On this occasion they were sitting in the bar area and were in good spirits. They mocked my worried expression and concerns about the coup. They bought me a beer and explained how governments changed hands in Nigeria.

Since independence in 1960, under the first elected leader of the country, the wonderfully named Sir Abubakar Tafawa Balewa, the prospect of the military taking over at regular intervals has always existed. Sometimes democracy would be restored for a while, usually at the behest of foreign aid donors, and then the military would take over again, justifying their action on the basis of the high level of corruption of the politicians. Although this was usually true, the level of corruption was invariably exceeded by the military leaders who replaced them. Quite often it was one military leader who ousted another. The only good thing about all this was that the coups were usually bloodless and even the former leaders would often only suffer house arrest, rather than being lined up on the beach and shot, as has happened elsewhere in West Africa. Violence was certainly a feature of Nigerian politics, as exemplified by the Biafran war of secession in the late 1960s and by the regular bouts of tribal and religious hostilities, but the coups were often remarkably peaceful. In other words, it was a fairly regular happening and nothing to get worried about.

In fact, Bill and Ben, who had lived in the Congo for many years and had moved to Nigeria because it was 'safer', viewed the coup as nothing more than a rather welcome opportunity for a day off work and expected that everything would be back to normal the following day. Real life was a little more complicated than this but, in essence, they were right. Apart from a lot more roadblocks to make the usual diabolical traffic situation even worse, there were few visible signs of a military coup when we were allowed to leave the hotel the next day.

Relaxing a little due to the combined effects of beer and reassurance, I now feigned nonchalance and insisted that I had never been worried anyway. I excused myself from the company of Bill and Ben, who were embarking upon a hard day's drinking, even though it was only mid-morning, and walked around the inner courtyard area of the hotel to see what was going on.

While in the bar I had been vaguely aware of loud music in the background, and I now found that a Scandinavian pop group had taken up residence on the hotel's open-air stage and were belting out 'Feed the World', made famous by Band Aid the previous year. In fact, the group had obviously been greatly affected by Bob Geldof and his efforts on behalf of the starving people of Ethiopia, because their entire, and very limited, repertoire seemed to consist of songs connected with Band Aid and Live Aid, the latter having been an enormous success the previous month, July 1985.

The pop group, perhaps overcome with an 'entertain the troops' mentality or maybe just glad of the opportunity to practise in front of an audience, proceeded to play their few songs time and again throughout the day. The line 'Do they know it's Christmas?' seemed particularly inappropriate on a sweltering August day in West Africa. Nobody had the heart to ask them to shut up, not even Bill and Ben, who despised Band Aid and Live Aid. As old Africa hands they said that such efforts to help Ethiopia were entirely misplaced and counterproductive until the Marxist Mengistu regime was removed.

One group of residents who did appreciate the efforts of the pop group were a team of about a dozen engineers from Yugoslavia who were installing equipment in a new Tito-inspired factory on the outskirts of Lagos. In contrast to my own reaction to the coup, the Yugoslavs could not believe their luck – an extra day's holiday, a fully stocked bar, live music and large numbers of prostitutes who were trapped in the hotel like all the residents and staff. Seemingly oblivious to the health risks involved, the Yugoslavs kept the girls busy all day, and not just as dancing partners.

Killing time while waiting for the appointed hour of the broadcast to the nation by the new leader, I was wandering around the hotel grounds, watching the geckos scampering up vertical walls with the benefit of their adhesive toes, when a very large pot plant said to me in a posh English accent, 'Would you like to take me upstairs to your room?' Fearing that I had drunk one too many beers in the midday sun, and worrying that a pink elephant might be the next thing to appear, I was relieved to see a young lady emerge from behind the plant. Regaining my composure, I politely declined her invitation and was about to move away when I realised that there was something that distinguished her from all the other ladies engaged in the same profession. She looked much the same as the other girls, with her excessive makeup and tight-fitting clothes, but her accent was completely different.

'If you don't mind me asking, where did you learn to speak English?' I said.

'Actually,' she said in tones reminiscent of a Priscilla at a hunt ball, 'I was educated in the UK'.

'Where?' I asked, genuinely interested to find out more.

'Oh, you wouldn't have heard of the place' she said, 'it was a small private school in north Wales'.

'Not by any chance Clarendon School?' I asked.

'Crikey, yes!' she replied in astonishment.

So it was that I found out that my wife and Devina had gone to the same school. They were not contemporaries, but it was a coincidence. There is a sad side to the story, because Devina had fallen on hard times after her businessman father had lost a lot of money in the notorious cement importing scam of some years before, but as she said herself, it was her choice to earn her living in this way. Devina also saw the funny side of the story, and so has everyone else I have relayed it to with the single exception of my wife's mother. Dear Edwina, who had scrimped and saved, together with her husband, to send her daughter to a religious boarding school in north Wales so that she would be removed from the diversions and temptations of Birmingham, had actually sent her to the same school as a future prostitute. Edwina was deeply shocked, and I was advised never to mention it again.

Still with a little time on my hands before the broadcast, I wandered over to some stalls where Nigerian handicrafts were on sale. A little thing like a coup had not stopped these sellers from coming to work, particularly on a day when they had virtually a captive market. I am not a great purchaser of furniture, ornaments and handicrafts because my wife says that the house is full enough of such stuff already. Also, I generally make it an absolute rule not to buy anything in the vicinity of large hotels because prices escalate with added proximity, but some days previously I had seen a wooden carved chair, in two interlocking pieces, on sale in one of the stalls, and it had really taken my fancy. Breaking all my usual rules, partly because I had not seen anything similar on sale elsewhere, I had begun price negotiations.

The seller welcomed me back like a long-lost brother, invited me to sit down on the chair I was interested in buying and praised me for not being taken in by all the fake Benin bronzes being offered for sale by his neighbours. He seemed to have had a lapse of memory about his last price offer, which was less than half his original asking price, but was happy to resume negotiations when I reminded him of the figure. At intervals during the protracted bargaining we chatted about other issues, including

173

the coup, and it was clear that there was general distrust of all politicians, whether military or civilian, and a fatalistic attitude that they were all out to line their own pockets. Accordingly, it made little difference to the seller and his friends who formed the government. Democratic selection was marginally better than rule by soldiers, but there was not much in it. At a very leisurely pace, we completed our bargaining and I became the proud owner of the chair.

Back in my room, I sat down in front of the television to become acquainted with the new ruler of the country. I wondered what small percentage of the population of 100 million had access to a TV. Some would have to make do with radio, and yet others in remote spots were probably sublimely ignorant that a coup had happened at all. The self-styled Chairman of the Armed Forces Ruling Council, Ibrahim Babangida, appeared and announced that his predecessor, Muhammad Buhari, Head of the Federal Military Government, had been removed. It was as if Bill and Ben had written the new leader's speech. He addressed the nation in English and said all the usual things about ending the corruption of the previous regime and ushering in a bright, new, clean administration. That was it, business as usual from the following day.

No doubt there were big changes in some quarters, not least among the ministers, but at the level I was operating, with senior civil servants and senior managers in the business community, life went on as normal the following day. The senior civil servants still had their air-conditioning turned up to Arctic proportions, the more senior the more Arctic, as a measure of status, which must explain why they wore thick three-piece suits. The expatriate businessmen were still totally obsessed by the subject of import licences, which had been almost the sole subject of conversation at the exclusive Metropolitan Luncheon Club the previous week when I had been invited along, and the coup was now being analysed in terms of its likely impact on import licence allocations.

One place where it was not business as usual was the airport. This remained closed for the following few days, presumably in an effort to stop certain people from leaving the country with their booty and to control the entry of Nigerians returning from abroad. Even at the best of times it was a nightmare to leave Lagos airport. Forget about having an OK ticket as a guarantee of a seat. No way – for every 100 OK tickets there would only be about 25-30 actual seats available, so the old hands always instructed rookie passengers to go to the airline office a few days before the flight and wait whatever number of hours was necessary in order to obtain a certified copy of the manifest. Armed with this document, together with a willingness to grease the necessary palms along the way, you stood a fighting chance of making it onto the plane.

As luck would have it, the airport reopened on the very day of my scheduled departure, three days after the coup. After spending innumerable hours at the Swissair office the previous day, I had acquired the necessary paperwork. The scheduled departure time was five minutes before midnight. The recommended check-in time was 7pm – five hours before. The taxi picked me up at the hotel at 3pm in order to leave time for the expected snail-like progress to the airport and to allow for the added interruptions of roadblocks at regular intervals, so I left the hotel nine hours before the flight time – such are the joys of business travel to exotic places, as I am always telling my unbelieving friends when they are lamenting that their own business travel extends to an occasional day trip to Luton. Give me Lagos rather than Luton any day, but it's not all beer and skittles, as my grandmother used to say.

With some trepidation I set off for the airport. I expected mega-hassles, and that is what I got. To some extent I was the author of my own misfortune because of the chair. Part of the deal with the seller was that he would package the 15kg monster in such a way that it would be easy to carry in addition to a suitcase and a briefcase. In the event, on the day of my departure, the packaging turned out to be maize flour sacks tied up with string. This had the combined effects of covering me in white powder while the string slowly sliced through my fingers. I quietly cursed the seller but it was too late to make any changes so I would have to make the best of a bad job.

The journey to the airport passed off as expected, but the scene that met my eyes on arrival was even worse than I had imagined. So many people were desperate to get on flights after the coup that the building was bursting at the seams. I stood outside the doors and watched a scene of absolute mayhem. Any notion of queuing had been totally abandoned as people pushed their way forward carrying great armfuls of luggage with children perched precariously on top. Some police and soldiers were trying, and failing, to keep order, until one of them had the bright idea of resorting to other methods.

Whether or not they had permission to use tear gas I do not know, but that was the means of crowd control they used. A little drastic perhaps, but it was extremely effective in clearing the check-in area and departure hall for quite some time. As far as I am aware no one was killed in the stampede, but I did not wait to check – I was busy attempting to run the 100 metres in 10 seconds flat while also disappearing in a cloud of maize dust. At various times of stress in airports such as JFK New York and Heathrow I have recommended similar direct action to the policemen on duty, but they always seem to be constrained by stricter rules.

The only other time I have been tear-gassed was in New Delhi in 1971, when I was caught between police lines and rioting students, At least in the case of Lagos airport, it was clear which way to run, although I was having second thoughts about the wisdom of buying the chair. I now bore a strong resemblance to a character on children's television in my childhood, Mr Pastry, who had many adventures that always ended up in him getting covered in flour. A long time later, when the dust had settled and the air had cleared, I was able to return to a crowded, but more orderly, departure hall. A much-prized boarding pass was eventually obtained.

There were still a couple of hours to kill before take-off and I spent the time chatting to a Dutchman who was a senior agronomist at the UN-funded International Institute of Tropical Agriculture, based at Ibadan, a couple of hours' drive north of Lagos. We had a common interest in certain crops, such as cassava; he was a renowned expert in their cultivation and I knew a great deal about their international markets. He travelled all over Africa and elsewhere, as did I. We agreed that all the efforts of people like us in the 'aid industry' to make a success of agricultural and other projects were undermined by political instability. The coup that we had just experienced, although much milder than a bloody civil war, still had the effect of destabilising most development efforts. Donor governments and agencies would take fright, planned projects would be aborted, existing projects might be curtailed and the new government would have its own priorities and international alliances, which might well be at odds with those of its predecessor. Even more important, in economic development terms, private sector companies, both local and foreign, would be dissuaded from investing because of the uncertainties. It would take years to get things back on an even keel, perhaps just in time for the next disruption.

Africa has been badly served by its leaders since independence. It is true that the continent suffers from many other problems including natural disasters, AIDS and other diseases, plus unfair trading practices imposed by the selfish rich world, but its own leaders have also been guilty of terrible crimes. We might forgive the misdeeds of incompetence and misplaced ideology committed by generally well-meaning leaders such as Nyerere and Kaunda, but we cannot forgive the crimes of greed, self-aggrandisement and cruelty committed by countless others. The rogues' gallery of disgraceful African leaders in the second half of the twentieth century is headed by such names as Bokassa, Amin, Mobutu and Taylor, but there are many others who have tried hard to emulate them. Some, such as Mugabe, have continued their vile regimes into the twenty-first century.

The coup in Nigeria in 1985 was only a blip on the African heart monitor, which has registered much greater fluctuations as a result of long-running and bloody civil wars and general political mayhem. Nevertheless, such blips can stymie development efforts for years to come. Good and stable government is an essential pre-requisite for real development. Perhaps only Botswana can be said to have been well governed since independence, but Ghana, South Africa and others show some signs of improvement. Even

Nigeria after 1999, under the democratically elected President Olusegun Obasanjo, displayed some encouraging signs. Indeed, the military have not taken over since that time and there has been a succession of elected leaders, although not without many incidents of serious civil unrest.

On arrival back at Heathrow I was subjected to the lengthiest search by customs officials I have ever encountered, even longer than on return trips from Jamaica and Afghanistan, both of which are certainties for a good grilling. I suppose that a dishevelled individual just arrived from Nigeria, covered in white powder and carrying some suspicious-looking luggage, was always going to be a candidate for questioning. I optimistically headed for the green channel but was soon diverted to an inspection room where uniformed officials spent an eternity tapping every inch of my chair in the expectation of finding some secret compartment. But it was worth the effort, because ever since then the 'Nigerian deckchair', as it became known by my family, has had pride of place in my office at home where it remains to this day, frequently sat on by my grandchildren.

My next visit to Nigeria was in 1989 and provided an eye-opener into a fascinating sub-sector of the commercial world in Africa – that of the Asian-owned businesses. My first conscious knowledge that a lot of businesses in Africa are Asian owned arrived in 1969 when I went to live and work in a remote part of Zambia. Virtually all the shops and other businesses in the local town of Kasama, in Northern Province, were Asian owned. Even the little general store in the village where I lived, where you could buy cigarettes, Coca Cola and Fray Bentos corned beef, was owned by an Asian family. When I strayed further afield, down to the Durban area of South Africa and up to the towns and cities of East Africa, I was amazed to find that large numbers of people of Asian extraction exerted a very strong influence over the commercial life of those countries.

A few years later, in 1972, when Idi Amin expelled 60,000 Asians from Uganda in an act of ethnic cleansing, which was also a misguided attempt to encourage African ownership of Ugandan businesses, the whole world came to realise the extent of the Asian role in some African countries and the difficulties they were experiencing in the post-independence period. A part of these difficulties was self-inflicted because, to put it mildly, some of the Asians could be very rude and arrogant in their dealings with their African staff and customers, as I had first witnessed in Kasama, but others recognised the realities of the new situation and behaved accordingly. Asians also had the reputation of trying to flout exchange control regulations by salting away their money in European bank accounts. Many incidents, such as the arrest of a gentleman from Malawi who was caught exporting a refrigerator stuffed full of dollar bills, added to this perception. But nothing could justify the actions of Amin. Perhaps to spite him, many Asian families made great successes of their new lives in the UK and elsewhere, often starting businesses that have developed into substantial enterprises, while at the same time Uganda suffered greatly from the loss of their entrepreneurial skills.

Asian families in West Africa were much less numerous and conspicuous than those in East Africa, but they still exerted an important influence in local business affairs. In 1989 one of the largest Asian-owned companies operating in Nigeria commissioned the consultancy company I worked for to carry out an assessment of new business opportunities in the country.

The client company already had substantial commercial interests in Nigerian retailing, wholesaling, textiles and cotton production. Aware that many companies in East Africa were enjoying success in the export to Europe of fruits, vegetables and flowers, the company wanted us to examine the opportunities in Nigeria for expanding into the horticultural sector.

If a similar study had been undertaken for one of the aid agencies it would probably have taken months, culminating in the presentation of a three-volume report. We were offered no such timetable. The fieldwork visit to Nigeria was to last only 10 days, even though we were expected to visit several regions, and a short report was expected one week later. Fortunately I had worked for private sector clients at intervals throughout my career and was not fazed by such a schedule, but some of my 'aid industry' colleagues would have been horror struck.

To make matters more challenging, we had to cover the vast distances by car rather than by plane. It was January, in the middle of the dry season, and the Harmattan wind was blowing down from the Sahara, causing many airports to close due to dust and visibility problems. After one night in Lagos at the Eko Meridien, under new ownership but not much changed from 1985, we set off northwards, leaving the steamy heat of the original 'white man's grave' in the south, with its low-lying lagoons and mangrove swamps, and heading towards Kano in the north, passing through rainforest, savannah and then semi-desert.

After a marathon drive, our first night was spent at Abuja, which was destined to become the new federal capital in 1991. Lagos was considered to be too overcrowded and too southern. Abuja was almost plumb centre in the country, in a beautiful setting with views over the savannah. That was the good news but the bad news was that almost no one in government, diplomatic and business circles wanted to relocate to a building site in 'the bush'. Efforts to encourage this relocation had fallen on deaf ears and explained why Abuja was like a ghost city. Many buildings and roads had been completed, reminding me of an African Milton Keynes, which is not surprising as I understand that town planners from MK were involved, probably on a British aid project. We stayed in almost splendid isolation at the Abuja Hilton and the hotel staff were about the only human beings that I saw in our short stay in the town. The contrast with Lagos, where we had stayed the previous night, could not have been greater.

From Abuja we travelled on to the Muslim north, to Kaduna and Kano, then across the Jos Plateau to Yola. The hotels and rest houses we stayed in were much less luxurious than the Abuja Hilton. Also, they got our reservations wrong in every case. Throughout Africa I have become familiar with my name being reversed so that Stephen Jones often becomes Jones Stephen or some variant such as Jon Steven. This had never been a problem in the past but now I was travelling with a colleague, an agriculturalist named John Stevens. He was an old Africa hand who had also become familiar, on occasion, with being called Steven John. Our efforts to disentangle the confusion at various hotel reception desks proved futile, so we just accepted being called any name that vaguely resembled our own.

Nigeria is not blessed with sensational scenery to compare with other parts of Africa but the Jos Plateau, rising to 1800 metres (6000 feet) is about as good as it gets. Travelling across the plateau, passing signs to the village of Bum, I was reminded of a place in Sierra Leone called Bum chiefdom in Bonth District. There are a surprising number of places in the world named Bum. A couple are in Nigeria, which some people might say is appropriate, and others are to be found in such places as Afghanistan, Burma, Azerbaijan and Honduras. There is even somewhere in Venezuela with the charming name of Bum Bum. How glad I am that I do not hail from such a place. 'And where do you come from?' 'Bum.' 'Well I only asked'. A lot of offence could be given in this way.

We were accompanied on our mad rush round Nigeria by one of the senior managers of the client company. Very appropriately his name was Sunny, because this accurately described his disposition. Like several of the managers of the company, he had been recruited in India, because the proprietors found that recruiting African graduates with the same work ethic was difficult. Sunny's appetite for hard work was insatiable. He spent all the long hours in the car either reading the various reports we had brought with us or cross-examining us, in the politest possible way, on our knowledge of how horticultural export industries had been established in other countries. Sunny was fascinated by the experience of Kenya, which had built a successful export industry based on flowers, green beans and exotic fruits, and he thought this could be replicated in Nigeria.

While in the north, we visited one of the few existing private horticultural export projects already established in Nigeria. This was a specialist mangetout project in the vicinity of Kano with easy access to the airport for air freighting the precious cargo to the UK for onward distribution to supermarket shelves. Although I was very familiar with visiting high-value export projects in many countries, this particular venture seemed bizarre in the extreme, with a large area of semi desert in northern Nigeria being irrigated to produce vast quantities of mangetout for dinner parties in Hampstead and Tunbridge Wells.

Thankfully, by the time we reached Yola on the Nigeria-Cameroon border, the airport was open and we were able to fly back to Lagos rather than continue our whistle-stop tour of Nigeria by car. It had been fascinating, but you can have enough of a good thing. We attended a few debriefing meetings in Lagos before departing for home. My return flight to London also departed at five minutes before midnight, as in 1985. As a measure of some improvements in the traffic and the security situations, we only had to leave the hotel for the airport five hours before departure rather than the nine hours of 1985. On this occasion I was determined not to carry any bulky parcels, just in case.

CHAPTER 10

AROUND THE WORLD WITH CHILEAN CHICKEN, 1985

'You have never played polo' repeated Juan-Estaban incredulously, 'but Prince Charles plays polo'. When I explained that not only had I never played polo but I had never ridden a horse in my life, the assembled members of the Santiago Polo Club fell about in amusement and astonishment. As members of Chile's privileged upper class it was as natural for them to ride horses as it was for me to ride a bicycle.

It was Saturday November 9th 1985, and Juan-Estaban had just collected me from the airport. Totally ignoring the fact that I had spent the last 24 hours on a succession of planes carrying me from Switzerland to Chile, via Paris and Rio de Janeiro, he had imagined that the first thing I would want to do on arrival, even before dropping off my luggage at a hotel, was to play a quick chukka or two. Greatly taken aback at my complete lack of equine capabilities, having previously imagined that every Englishman worth his salt would share the British Royal Family's addiction to horsy sports, he now motioned me to sit down in the spectator area until his game was finished.

Although I would rather have been tucked up in bed catching up on much-needed sleep, I now had my first opportunity to observe the microcosm of Chilean society set out before me, and very revealing it was too. My reading matter on the plane had included various official pamphlets obtained from the Chilean embassy in London. One of these spoke about the Chilean population being 'people of one indigenous origin'. This struck me as odd. My only previous visit to South America had been to Ecuador where, in the environs of Quito, the Indian population with their wonderful bowler hats and pigtails had fascinated me. I knew that people of Amerindian origins were far fewer in Chile, heavily outnumbered by those of European descent, but they existed, and there were also large numbers of people of mixed race.

The evidence was all around me. Whereas all the players riding polo ponies were clearly of European origin, the grooms and other attendants all looked like they were descended from the Incas. Similarly, the expensively dressed spectators, wearing designer sunglasses to protect them from the summer sun and sipping excellent Chilean wine in the sumptuous surroundings of the polo club, appeared to be of pure European stock, whereas the waiters, gardeners and other workers did not.

Juan-Estaban rode over at the end of the game, mallet in hand. 'Did you enjoy my play?' he enquired, 'Fantastic', I lied, having been far more preoccupied with my mini social survey of the Chilean class system. I had also spent some time musing on what on earth I was doing in Chile in the first place.

The simple answer was that I had been retained by the International Trade Centre UNCTAD-GATT, to give it its full name, to act as an adviser to a Chilean trade mission that was about to set off round the world to promote Chilean poultry products and other agricultural exports. The difficult part to fathom was why ITC had selected me for the job. I seemed to be singularly unqualified for the task, given that I spoke barely a word of Spanish and had little previous experience of poultry products. But professional consultants are paid by their companies to seek out work and not find reasons for turning it down, so here I was.

I had just come from two days of briefing meetings at the ITC headquarters in Geneva. An organisation that was already reasonably well known to me from my time at the institute, it specialised in helping developing countries increase their exports and was an offshoot of two much grander Geneva–based parent organisations – the United Nations Conference on Trade and Development (UNCTAD) and the General Agreement on Tariffs and Trade (GATT), which later became the World Trade Organization.

I had been on the ITC 'roster of experts' for a number of years, but this was the one and only time that I was approached to carry out a consultancy assignment. For all the vast number of ITC projects around the world that I was well-qualified to undertake, I was never approached, but I was told by Mr Ruibal, the desk officer for Chile, that I was considered indispensable for this particular assignment. Goodness knows why, but I had enough experience of international aid organisations not to expect rational explanations. I also had limited expectations about the usefulness of the briefing meetings, which was just as well because they were useless. They consisted of meeting a number of ITC officers so that ticks could be put in boxes to say that I had met them, but that was all.

My terms of reference said that I was to go to Chile to work with the export promotion organisation PROCHILE, which was organising a trade mission to visit selected major importing countries of frozen chicken and other products. The rather interesting and disparate selection of places to be visited consisted of Egypt, Singapore, Hong Kong and Japan. I was to accompany the mission, providing advice on marketing and business methods in these very different economies. I was invited to spend a couple of hours in the ITC library to collect data on trade statistics and other information, then I was on my own. I was to fly to Santiago immediately and return to Geneva in five weeks' time to report on a successful mission, but not to bother anyone at ITC in the meantime.

The doubting Thomases among my friends in London thought that the frozen chicken cover story was no more convincing than the one about desiccated coconut and speculated that I was involved in a covert operation, possibly to source arms for the Pinochet regime. In further flights of fancy, the espionage conspiracy theorists proposed that Mrs Thatcher could not openly give rewards to her buddy for his support against Argentina in the recent (1982) Falklands War and so had to resort to hidden methods. I protested that it would be difficult to find a more unlikely arms dealer than myself, that I was working for the United Nations and not the British Government and that I was implacably opposed to the extreme right-wing Pinochet government which had a nasty habit of making its opponents disappear off the face of the earth, but all to no avail. My friends had an annoying habit of tapping the sides of their noses while giving knowing looks.

While in Santiago and, later, in the company of my trade mission colleagues on our world tour, I had to be very circumspect about expressing my political views concerning General Pinochet, because the whole subject was still red raw to most Chileans. That other famous September 11th, the one in 1973 when democratically elected President Salvador Allende was violently removed from power in a CIA-backed coup, still seemed to be a sharply poignant memory. At the time of my visit the dictatorship of General Augusto Pinochet had already lasted for 12 years and would continue for another five, but the mere mention of Allende's name was usually enough to induce collective apoplexy among my contacts.

Part of the reason the political climate was so electric was because the '*extremista*' were still letting off bombs, indeed a small one went off in Santiago near my hotel during my stay. Also, there was a lot of international media coverage about torture and human rights violations. But among my contacts, who were certainly not a representative cross-section of the 14 million Chilean people, being drawn as they were from the business and professional classes, the main sins of Allende were economic. They blamed him for trying to introduce Marxist economic policies which would have been catastrophic for the country, and they congratulated Pinochet on ushering in free-market reforms that would make all Chileans, and particularly themselves, more prosperous. I was in broad agreement with these economic arguments, although I tried to suggest that economic progress did not have to go hand in hand with state murder, torture and loss of democratic freedoms. But for them the human rights violations were either ignored or considered to be an acceptable price to pay.

Many years later, in 1997, when I visited Chile again, I found that these were still subjects of daily conversation, although the debate was more evenly balanced, with more people prepared to acknowledge the mistakes of Pinochet's 17 years in power. I still found no one with a good word to say for Allende, but this was almost certainly because I had no opportunities during these brief visits to meet anyone from outside the professional classes.

Not surprisingly, when I met the members of the forthcoming trade mission, they all appeared to be of pure European descent, at least moderately wealthy and some very wealthy and of, let's say, conservative political views. I was fascinated to learn that they identified themselves closely with their European origins, describing themselves as German Chileans, English Chileans or Spanish Chileans, to the extent that they sent their children to specialist German or English schools and tended to socialise and marry within their clans. Apart from Juan-Estaban, who worked for PROCHILE and would be the official representative on the trip, the others were all either owners or directors of agribusiness companies engaged in the poultry or processed fruit sectors.

On most aid projects in different parts of the world, particularly in Africa, I have usually felt like a rich man amongst the poor, but in this case I was the poor relation, particularly in the company of a charming chap of German extraction named Werner who explained that his father had once been one of the biggest individual landowners in the world before the government instituted a land redistribution scheme in the pre-

Allende era. The family were not reduced to penury, however, since they still controlled several thousand hectares of land plus food processing plants, hotels and other investments. The other members of the mission did not match this level of wealth, but they were all affluent.

I tried to get my mind round the concept of international aid funds, in this case money channelled through the United Nations network, being used to further the business interests of this group. True, the individual mission members, or their companies, were funding some of their own expenses, but there was also a subsidy element from the UN. Was this a legitimate use of aid funds? Some people in the 'aid industry' would have been horrified. Their view, which has been widely adopted in more recent times, is that all aid funds should be spent directly on the poorest in society. At a superficial level it is easy to sympathise with this belief, particularly where help is being given to individuals or small groups, but when the 'pro-poor' or poverty-focused approach is applied to large-scale aid projects there is often a high failure rate.

Indeed, as my 'aid industry' career progressed I was becoming increasingly aware that the success rate of aid projects in general was alarmingly low. I was developing the view that poverty reduction on a grand scale, as achieved in many parts of Southeast Asia in the second half of the twentieth century, had little to do with aid, and instead was usually based on a strong business development foundation, allied to growth in international trade. Over the years my belief in this view has been reinforced. Certain countries, such as Nepal, with few opportunities to engage in significant international trade, would always need aid support but many others were better candidates for the 'trade rather than aid' approach. This requires that more developed countries open up their markets to Third World exports which sometimes happens but is often not the case. It also suggests that aid money, in some cases, might be best spent on helping poor countries to develop their exports.

On the face of it, my job with the Chilean trade mission should have been a good example of aid funds being spent in this way. But this led to consideration of another important issue: how to ensure that the benefits were fairly shared at all levels of society. I had to admit that in this particular case there did not seem to be a great likelihood that the benefits of selling increased quantities of Chilean exports would trickle down to the poorest members of society. Of course, some agricultural labourers and processing factory workers would encounter increased employment opportunities, but their remuneration levels were desperately low and it seemed that the majority of the benefits would probably remain with the swimming pool-owning elite.

Chilean business leaders were not renowned for their generosity; in fact they were capable of some rather nasty forms of exploitation, not only of workers but also of consumers. One example illustrates the point. When I questioned the senior executives employed by the frozen chicken companies about the high retail price of their product in the domestic market, suggesting that they would not be price competitive on the world stage, they replied that there was no problem because the local price was kept artificially high by an illegal cartel arrangement operated by the leading firms. They were even quite proud of the sophisticated demand/supply analysis they used that enabled them to control retail prices by pooling data and manipulating supply to the shops. Such activities did not suggest a business culture that would have readily distributed to the poor the benefits resulting from increased exports and this gave me some misgivings about the use of UN funds in this case.

Nevertheless, I was determined to do a professional job of assisting the trade mission to the best of my ability and joined in the efforts to bring some order to the chaos of the existing arrangements. Communication alone was a major headache. Today we take for granted instantaneous telephone and email contact but back in 1985, even in Europe, we were still only slowly emerging from the era of the telex and entering that of the fax. Imagine being in Santiago trying to confirm and coordinate meeting arrangements in Egypt, Singapore, Hong Kong and Japan, plus making the associated flight and hotel bookings. Of course, PROCHILE had been making preparations for quite some time but on each occasion that somebody in one country announced a change of plan it resulted in a chain reaction throughout the whole programme.

I will be forever grateful to Rosa, who worked for a travel agency in Santiago and changed airline bookings again and again with great good humour. She explained that her husband had once spent three months in hospital in Manchester and she felt a debt of gratitude to the British. She cheerfully accommodated such modest changes of plan as going round the world in an easterly direction starting with Cairo instead of going round the world in a westerly direction starting with Tokyo.

The rest of my time in Santiago was spent making briefing visits to various poultry units and fruit-processing factories. The latter held no surprises because I had visited many similar plants in many countries. The poultry units were more of a novelty for me and such visits would be repeated in all the countries we visited on our world tour. In the space of five weeks I saw more poultry than I had imagined existed in the whole world. We visited breeding units, broiler units (for meat) and layer units (for eggs). Some were owned by multinational companies such as Arbor Acres, while others were relatively small enterprises. The smell was universally dreadful, but the prize for the worst smell in the poultry world goes to a broiler unit on the outskirts of Cairo on a hot day. The worst sight was any one of the layer units using battery cages where the pathetic birds were crammed into a tiny space and passed the time by pecking each other to death. I have few animal liberation sympathies, but ending battery farming is a cause that I do support.

There are two particular poultry images that stick in my memory. The first is a slaughterhouse in the Central Valley area of Chile, not far from Santiago, where the chickens about to be killed were suspended upside down, attached by their feet to a conveyor belt system. As each slaughterman slit the throat of a suspended chicken, one after another, he uttered a few words. I asked what they were saying. It transpired that the meat was destined for export to the Middle East and, in accordance with Islamic practices, the slaughterer was required to say 'Allah O Akbar' (God is great) as he slit each throat. Apparently religious inspectors from the importing country travelled all the way to Chile on a fairly regular basis to check that the various stipulations were being rigidly applied. I asked if the Chilean workers had any idea what they were saying and why, but only got a shrug in answer.

The second enduring image is of a chick sexer at work. On days when I felt fed up with my occupation as a consultant, I reminded myself that I could work as a chick sexer. I do not wish to suggest that this is not an important or worthwhile calling but just that I would not like to do it. The chick sexer spends all day, working at great speed, looking at the private parts of little fluffy chicks and putting them in the male or female box. It is very specialised work. I was shown what to look for but was totally unable to spot the difference, even after a lengthy inspection.

After about a week of frantically rearranging the itinerary, we were ready to depart. The first port of call was Egypt. Santiago to Cairo was not a frequently used route and involved a journey time of 31 hours, again with transfers in Rio and Paris. Eventually the bedraggled trade mission emerged from the lengthy passport and customs procedures into the chaotic light of day of Cairo arrivals hall. From this point onwards the Chileans endured collective culture shock. Although many members of the mission had travelled quite widely, they had never visited anywhere like this before. Crowds, heat, dust, noise and a general state of chaos engulfed them. They found the sheer weight of numbers of people very intimidating and were not surprised to be told that Egypt's population at the time was increasing at the alarmingly fast rate of one million people every nine months.

The Chileans were accustomed to the ordered surroundings of Santiago, which could easily be mistaken for a city in Europe if you averted your eyes from the shanty towns on the outskirts. But Cairo was much bigger, more chaotic and certainly not ordered. On the journey to the hotel they were particularly struck by the traffic on the roads, almost literally in fact, as kamikaze motorists attempted to squeeze their vehicles through non-existent gaps. They enquired if it was compulsory to keep one's hand on the horn the whole time because the deafening noise gave weight to this theory. They were astonished by the vast numbers of traffic policemen and the fact that they were totally ignored by all road users.

The sumptuous surroundings of the Marriott Hotel, on the banks of the Nile, offered some reassurance to the Chileans and provided the degree of luxury with which they were more familiar. The hotel, however, provided me with a problem – I could not afford to stay there. This situation arose from the ludicrous system of daily allowances, or 'per diems' as they are usually known in the aid world. It is argued that individuals cannot be trusted simply to claim back their actual hotel, food and other expenses because many people would abuse the system. Therefore, the United Nations has set rates for every city in the world and each individual working for a part of the UN receives that rate whether he/she spends it or not. This results in some aid workers or consultants staying in doss houses or with friends and pocketing a tidy sum. To make matters more complicated, many of the other aid institutions have their own set rates that are different from the UN rates. For example, there are World Bank rates and even the British ministry responsible for overseas aid has its own rates.

The system of per diems leads to many anomalies. The rates often get out of date due to devaluations, other currency movements or just through bureaucratic incompetence, so that in some cities you can afford to live very comfortably while in others you barely have enough money to eat properly. My problem on this trade mission was that the Chileans chose to stay in more luxurious surroundings than I could afford on UN rates. In order to avoid the hassle of staying in cheaper hotels, my company helped a bit and, aware of my dilemma, a few of the Chileans were generous in paying for some of my incidental expenses, particularly drinks in hotel bars, where the prices are always extortionate. Again, this was an interesting reversal of normal practice; I would often subsidise colleagues from developing countries, but in this case I was on the receiving end of the generosity of others.

The methods of doing business in Egypt proved to be a further culture shock for the Chileans. As enthusiasts for unrestrained private enterprise, they were more at home with the business methods employed in the countries we were yet to visit on the trade mission. In many sectors of the Egyptian economy at this time, private enterprise took a back seat. Government-controlled buying organisations with monopoly powers organised the large-scale importing of many commodities. Just imagine the chaos if a government company in the UK, staffed by civil servants, was responsible for import contracts for frozen chicken and other commodities instead of the supermarkets or food companies; it would be a recipe for disaster.

The Egyptian system revolved around government contracts, bureaucratic delays and shady facilitation fees. The authorities encouraged foreign suppliers to operate through local agents, all of whom seemed to drive expensive Mercedes, presumably paid for by various dubious deals. A cynic might suggest that the whole system of government control of the buying process, ostensibly to guard against exploitation by big foreign suppliers, was actually a perfect cover for backhanders and other corrupt practices. It would be some years in the future before the Egyptian government, like many others, learned that somewhere between unrestrained capitalism and tight government control there is a sensible middle path where government confines itself to enforcing regulations but leaves free market competition to get on with the job of organising the efficient and cost effective supply of products to consumers.

After the initial shock, the Chileans were starting to enjoy Cairo. They discovered that there was a well-educated business and professional class, rather like themselves, who were very hospitable. There were many invitations to dinner, often at 10pm or later, according to Egyptian custom. We also managed to find time for some of the sensational tourist attractions. The most memorable visit in the city was to the Tutankhamun room at the Egyptian Museum in Tahir Square where, at that time, the mask and other breath-taking exhibits were wonderfully jumbled together in a little room, probably much as they were inside the tomb, instead of being put on show in spacious and sterile surroundings as I have seen them displayed in touring exhibitions in other parts of the world.

On the outskirts of Cairo, we visited the Pyramids of Giza. After walking round the Sphinx and viewing the pyramids in the distance, we were persuaded, like so many others, that a camel ride was the only way to take a closer look at the modest resting places of Khufu (Cheops), Khafre (Chephren) and Menkaure (Mycerinus). This was tolerable, because we were all inexperienced camel riders and simply plodded along in the control of the camel owner. On our return one of the Chileans noticed a place where there were horses for hire. My heart sank. My protestations that I would be perfectly happy to wait for them while they played cowboys round the pyramids were totally ignored. They insisted that I come with them and promised that we would go no faster than a trot. They lied.

Juan-Estaban took the reins of my horse and helpfully suggested that I hold on tight. 'Grip with the knees' he kept saying. Once I was in the saddle, we set off across the desert like one of Genghis Khan's invading armies mounting a charge. We thundered round the pyramids for what seemed like hours, scattering tourists in all directions, with the Chileans whooping with glee and greatly enjoying my discomfiture. This remains the one and only time in my life when I have ridden, or rather clung on to, a horse.

Back in the more sedate surroundings of the Marriott, we met one of the Chileans looking very glum. Pablo was the dandy of the group, always immaculately dressed, with a gigantic suitcase for his clothes that would have done justice to Zsa Zsa Gabor. Whereas I had brought one suit with me for all occasions, Pablo seemed to have a different one for every day of the trip. On this particular day he had passed on the visit to Giza, deciding to go shopping instead. The joke among other members of the group was that he was running low on suits and had heard that he could get them made in 24 hours in the bazaar. Indeed, a couple of weeks later in Hong Kong he did have some new suits made and had to buy another suitcase to carry all his purchases back home. Anyway, whatever he was shopping for in Cairo, he decided that he needed to change money into Egyptian pounds. Unwisely he accepted the invitation of one of the many individuals on the street, who approached all foreigners with the greeting 'Change money?' Perhaps Pablo was thinking that the black market, money-changing scene in Cairo would be like that in Santiago. I had been amazed the previous week when I had been led into an underground office at the Santiago stock exchange, where men in smart suits had openly offered me the 'parallel rate' of 208 pesos to the US dollar instead of the official rate of 185. This was the most sophisticated black market I had ever seen and I had experienced quite a few. The insistence of many governments, particularly in developing countries, on trying to maintain unrealistic official rates of exchange encouraged the emergence of currency black markets in many countries. I was familiar with changing money in this way in order to eke out the inadequate budgets I was often given, always exercising due caution so as not to be hit over the head and robbed.

Pablo's experience was not violent, but he had fallen for one of the oldest tricks in the book. He had followed the man down a confusing network of alleyways and into the back room of a shop. In a darkened little office he had been enticed by a very attractive black market rate. On handing over his dollars and being given bundles of Egyptian pounds tightly held together by elastic bands he was ushered out into the alleyways and led back to a main street before being waved on his way. It was only later, when he came to pay for one of his purchases, that he found that - you guessed it – each bundle had genuine pounds on the top and bottom but blank pieces of paper in between.

The Egyptian government had also devised a way of separating foreign visitors from their dollars. In 1985 it was required that every visitor must change a given amount of foreign exchange into Egyptian pounds for every day of his stay. This meant that you could end up with a considerable surplus of pounds. Knowing that it was not a convertible currency in the outside world I had tried to change pounds into dollars at a bank in Cairo shortly before our departure and been told that I could only do this at the change counter at the airport. There I was also told that the government did not allow any reconverting of pounds. I consoled myself with the thought that, as a last resort, I could spend my surplus money in the duty-free shops in the departure area but, as the final part of the government's cunning plan, these shops displayed signs saying that they were only allowed to accept hard currency.

Seriously miffed by this and with a wallet full of Egyptian pounds, I boarded the plane for Singapore. My question to the cabin crew as to whether they would accept Egyptian currency for duty free items was met with hysterical laughter, but good old Singaporean efficiency later came to the rescue. I have not always been a great admirer of Singapore, having likened it at times to a floating department store, but even I must admit that it is efficient, particularly after coming directly from a chaotic place such as Cairo.

There was no need for a currency black market, because Singapore dollars were fully convertible and no attempt was made to prop up an unrealistic rate. It seemed as if every street corner had an officially sanctioned exchange bureau. The first day after our arrival, at one such open-air counter, almost as a joke, I asked the man behind the desk what rate he would give for Egyptian pounds. To my astonishment he did not make rude gestures or set his dog on me but made one quick phone call, apologising that he did not have the current rate in his head, and then quoted me a very acceptable rate. Feigning calmness, I fumbled in my briefcase for the pounds, shovelled the notes on to his counter and ran away with the precious Singapore dollars before he could change his mind.

Somehow this epitomised the differences between the Egyptian and Singaporean economic systems, the former being closed and rigidly controlled while the latter was open and much closer to free trade. In spite of the fact that the Singaporean newspapers at the time were full of tales of woe about recession and collapsing share prices, the open system seemed to work much better. This applied to the frozen chicken business, as well as all the other agri-export products we were promoting. In places such as Singapore and Hong Kong, import companies made their buying decisions on rational bases such as price, quality and delivery times rather than arbitrary bases such as which import agent had greased which palms when a tender was announced. That is not to say that bribery and corruption do not exist in Singapore and Hong Kong, of course they do, but an open and transparent system provides fewer opportunities.

I was beginning to realise that accompanying a trade mission was money for old rope compared to my usual consultancy work. Instead of dashing around like a headless chicken collecting information for a marketing or feasibility study and then having to write a very comprehensive report, I was now simply advising on different aspects of international marketing in each location and I knew that ITC expected no more than a few pages of final report on my return. Advising on marketing headless chickens was better than being one. Better still, as part of an official trade mission I was invited to all the dinners and banquets along the way. The pinnacle of these was held at the Jockey Club in Hong Kong, where we were treated to the most sumptuous Chinese meal I have ever tasted. Everyone was happy except for Pablo, who said he would have preferred steak and French fries. To add insult to injury, a waiter spilt a little soy sauce down his new suit, but at least he had a dozen others to change into.

The opportunities for frozen chicken sales in Hong Kong were limited, the population preferring to buy live or fresh chickens in the famous wet markets. The colony could not supply its own needs for its five million population from the New Territories, so supplies were received from its massive neighbour, albeit on a rather erratic basis as businessmen on the mainland were still trying to get organised and shake off the fairly recent memories of the 'Cultural Revolution'. This was an interim period between the death of Mao only nine years previously and the eventual unification with China 12 years later, a prospect which was considered too remote to be worthy of serious discussion at the time of our visit in 1985.

One of the few opportunities for the Chileans in the Hong Kong market was to supply chicken feet. I have always failed to understand the Chinese penchant for this most unappetising of products, but each to their own. This curious partiality serves the international chicken business very well because of the favourable distribution of preferences for different parts of the animal in various parts of the world. West Europeans, for example, will eat chicken breast until it's coming out their ears, but as you travel further east the demand for chicken legs increases. In the early 1990s, after the fall of the Soviet Union, the two products from the American continent that arrived by the shipload in Russia were bananas from various parts of Latin America and chicken legs from the USA (known as Bush legs after the first President Bush). But most other parts of the world are happy to leave the feet to the Chinese.

Once in Japan, it was my own feet that presented a problem. They were too big. Whereas in Nepal some years previously my feet had been the subject of much hilarity by the local population, they now provided the Japanese with great embarrassment, even a minor diplomatic incident. We were about to embark upon a visit to a poultry slaughterhouse. My capacity for faking interest in yet another factory visit was growing thin, but I was buoyed by the hope that this would be the last one, perhaps in my whole life. We arrived by minibus from Tokyo and went through the usual elaborate greeting ceremony with the factory manager and his senior staff. Lots of bowing, exchanging business cards and gifts, then some more bowing before being taken to a cloakroom where we were supplied with white coats, hair nets and spotless white Wellington boots.

The average Japanese is about a foot shorter than me, with feet about five sizes smaller. The factory staff managed to fit all the Chileans with complete outfits and to supply me with a hair net and a white coat, which a clothing retailer might have described as 'snug'. It was fine so long as I did not attempt to move my arms from the 'hands up' position. The main problem was the boots, which were many sizes too small for my dainty feet. Apparently, it was unthinkable that I could be allowed to walk round in my ordinary shoes because that was forbidden by hygiene regulations and it was more than their jobs were worth to flout the rules. I volunteered to forgo the pleasures of seeing yet more foul (literally) smelling, dismembered carcasses and stay in the nice warm canteen, but that was also unthinkable for some reason. The apologies grew more agitated and the bowing got progressively lower until their noses were almost touching the ground. Frantic phone calls were made to some higher authority. Eventually the only solution they could come up with was to encase my feet in plastic bags tied at the shin. It was worth the humiliation of my dress to see the aghast looks on the faces of the factory workers as they were approached by a giant wearing plastic bags on his feet, a hairnet and his hands raised in the air as if someone had a gun in his back.

It is easy to laugh at Japanese bowing and legendary

politeness, but it provides a welcome and powerful contrast to the increasing yob culture of my own country. On another visit to Japan in 2002, I was pleased to note that the Japanese seemed as genuinely polite and considerate as ever. This even extended to teenagers and young people. One evening I was walking with a group of blind and visually impaired people of many nationalities back to our hotel where we were attending a Retina International conference at Chiba on Tokyo Bay. Suddenly we found ourselves engulfed by thousands of young people who had just spilled out of a pop concert in a nearby stadium. Although in great high spirits the crowd went to great lengths to avoid jostling our group, who were in danger of getting separated on a street busy with traffic as well as people. The remarkable thing was that this caring attitude was not just displayed by a few individuals but by everyone in a very large crowd. I fear that such sympathetic behaviour would not have been evident if the same group had strayed into the path of a pop concert crowd in London.

In addition to politeness, another recognised characteristic of the Japanese is conformity. The Chileans had already had a taste of this in Singapore when a coach had swept up in front of Raffles Hotel and disgorged its contents of about 60 identikit individuals wearing matching T-shirts and baseball caps. A banner was unfurled proclaiming in different languages that this was a Toyota factory holiday. They assembled behind the banner for the group photo and then ran back on to the bus. The Chileans, with memories of the relative anarchy of Cairo fresh in their minds, looked on in open-mouthed amazement. 'Some of them didn't even stop to look at Raffles', said Juan-Esteban.

Just when you think you are on the right road to understanding Japanese society with its politeness, conformity and efficiency, something happens to complicate matters. We arrived at Tokyo's Narita airport, previously the scene of many violent demonstrations by left-wing students and farmers in a failed attempt to stop it being built, to find that 'leftists' had disrupted all train services to and from the airport, preventing us from being met. We took very expensive taxis to the city centre, but the taxi drivers could not find the building we wanted because Tokyo, amazingly, has no proper system of naming and numbering its streets. For sheer inefficiency and inconvenience, our arrival in Tokyo was probably a worse experience than in Cairo.

Soon after our arrival the trade mission members received instruction in Japanese social and business etiquette from the trade attaché at the Chilean embassy. I was impressed that this Chilean gentleman spoke fluent Japanese and was surprised to be informed that he was General Pinochet's son-in-law. He explained how and when to bow and the procedure for giving and receiving business cards. Just handing over a card and putting the other person's in your pocket was not good enough. One should present one's own card with the name facing and on receiving the other person's card, make a great show of fascinated, close scrutiny.

The inscrutable Japanese way of doing business provided a further contrast with our experience in the three countries already visited. The first few days of meetings with Japanese importing organisations provided little hope for the Chileans that they were going to do any worthwhile business in Japan. We were, of course, treated very courteously, with fascinating trips to shrines, Mount Fuji, the bullet train and a banquet held at a golf club where the annual membership cost about half the equivalent of my annual salary. But the Chileans were disappointed that no real progress was being made, until that is, the night out with executives from Mitsui. Preliminary meetings had already taken place with this company, one of the giant trading companies known as *sogo shosha*, a grouping that includes other giants such as Mitsubishi and Sumitomo. A couple of days previously we had sat in one of Mitsui's vast offices looking out on a sea of identical-looking desks and people, all lined up with military precision, all eyes glued to the work on their desks, only looking up occasionally to the digital display on the ceiling to check the yen/dollar rate of exchange. When the bell rang to signal the end of the working day, not one person out of the many dozens on view moved a muscle. If anything, they bent lower over their work and would probably not go home for another two hours at least.

Our Mitsui hosts took us to dinner and then to a club. This was my first meeting with *geisha* girls and I was puzzled over what all the fuss was about. In the first place they appeared to be dressed in thick winter dressing gowns, as worn by aged aunts in England, with pillows attached to their backs. A less sexy form of attire would be difficult to imagine. Their faces were caked in make-up and they appeared to have stored their knitting needles in their hair, perhaps to avoid them getting lost. There was a lot of simpering small talk with every comment met with gales of tittering as if they were talking to the wittiest man in the world. One of our hosts tried to explain to me the difference between *geishas* and *oiran*, the latter word being translated as courtesans and the former being cultured ladies who acted as entertainers. I realised that I had succumbed to a common Western misconception about *geishas* but he did admit that the historical differences between the two professions were sometimes rather blurred.

Time passed, alcohol flowed, tittering continued and, it transpired, business was done. The senior man from Mitsui, to whom all the other employees obsequiously deferred, was transformed from a disinterested bystander into a business dynamo. He had clearly decided that the Chileans would make acceptable business partners. It was as if they had passed some kind of business and social test. By midnight he had accepted an invitation to visit Chile and had ordered a trial shipment of two containers of frozen chicken cuts. The Chileans were delighted; the whole trip had been worthwhile. I understand that Chilean exports to Japan were subsequently expanded as a result of our mission. I cling to the hope that some of the benefits did trickle down to the poorer members of Chilean society, but I will never know for sure.

CHAPTER 11

PAKISTAN, 1985 AND 1989/90

'Get down, they're shooting from my side', Chris and I said simultaneously, and then we realised that gunfire was coming from both sides. Five of us, including the driver, were crammed into a small taxi, together with our luggage, as it sped along the road from Karachi airport to the city centre. All four of the consultancy team were big men, either in height or weight, the largest weighing about 18 stone. Consequently, our frantic, yet futile, attempts to get our heads down were thwarted by the fact that we were packed into the taxi like sardines in a can. The most we could do was wriggle a bit while bending our heads as if in prayer. Come to think of it, a few prayers at this point might have been advisable. The only person who did manage to get his head down below the height of the windows was the driver, which was a bit worrying because the rest of us could see that the taxi was hurtling towards a palm tree, decoratively planted on the central reservation, until we politely alerted him to this fact and he took evasive action.

It was Friday 13th October 1989 and we were approaching the end of a two-month stay in Pakistan. Having been born one Friday 13th, I have never shared the superstition about this date being unlucky. Fortunately for me, my parents were not superstitious; otherwise they might have agreed with the lady in the next bed to my mother at the nursing home in London where I was born who was so upset at her baby's date of birth that she threatened to throw it into the nearby Grand Union Canal. Anyway, I can say that this date in 1989 was lucky because all of us escaped unhurt, although our collective aplomb was badly shaken.

We never did discover who was shooting at us, nor whether we were simply caught in the crossfire of two groups shooting at each other or whether we were the target. It was a fairly common occurrence in Karachi for one group or other to declare a 'wheel jam' whereby no vehicles were supposed to move, in an effort to bring the city to a standstill and demonstrate the power of the particular group in question. It was our misfortune that we had just flown in from Multan, a town in Punjab province, and were completely ignorant of the situation until the small number of taxi drivers still working at the airport explained what was going on and demanded five times the usual fare.

I was annoyed not to know who the gunmen were, but this was not unusual in Pakistan, where there were a bewildering number of warring factions. It is a country where ethnic, political and religious differences among the population of 110 million in 1989 could often be taken to extremes. The ethnic groups, in number order, include the Punjabis, Sindhis, Pathans (Pashtuns) and Baluchis. There are also the Mohajirs, a name given to those Muslims from India who fled to Pakistan at the time of partition in 1947, many of whom settled in the area around Karachi, which was transformed from a town of less than half a million to a city the size of London by the time of our visit.

All of these groups were represented not only in the population of Pakistan, but also in the population of Karachi, where they seemed to hate each other with a special vengeance. Any incident, such as a traffic accident or an accusation of inappropriate behaviour towards womenfolk, could quickly escalate out of control as the two sides faced up to each other, brandishing their Kalashnikov rifles (a must-have fashion item for the macho young men of the town). The police force was corrupt and useless, and they kept out of sight until the shooting died down and they could go back to collecting bribes in peace.

Enquiries made with Pakistani colleagues the following day elicited the view that we had probably been caught in the crossfire between groups of Pathans and Mohajirs, who were engaged in a bit of a war at that time, but it could easily have been other factions. In other words, it was no big deal and there were more important things to think about, like the latest cricket results.

Religious differences can also degenerate into violence, even though the nation's population is more than 95% Muslim. The Sunni-Shia divide was getting wider and bloodier at this time, partly as a result of the *jihad* against the Soviet occupation of Afghanistan supported by some Sunni groups in Pakistan. Things got worse in the 1990s in Afghanistan when the Sunni Taliban targeted Shia groups such as the Hazaras and the violence spilled over into Pakistan in places such as Quetta in Baluchistan province, close to the Afghan border. In March 2004, for example, there were reports of dozens of Shias being killed and wounded in Quetta by Sunni extremists.

As we travelled around the country in 1989, I kept an eye out for non-Muslim groups, interested to see how they fared in this environment. While on a farm visit in a remote part of Sindh province, our driver pointed out a group of pathetic-looking huts and said that this was one of the very few Hindu communities in the area. Presumably these families had ended up on the wrong side of the border in all the confusion at the time of partition, but I had no opportunity to find out more. One source at the time estimated that only 1.5% of the Pakistani population were Hindu, while 2.3% were Christian.

It is reported that a lot of Christians are poor bonded labourers and brick kiln workers, but the few Christians we ran across seemed to be relatively affluent. In fact, one very successful entrepreneur we met in Karachi, himself a Muslim, explained that he went out of his way to employ Christian office staff because they did not disappear to prayers several times a day. In particular, he preferred Christian female office workers, because he claimed they tended to be better educated and more businesslike. In more recent times, particularly after the invasion of Afghanistan by Western forces in 2001, there have been isolated yet murderous attacks on Christians and their churches, plus some Christians being accused and imprisoned under blasphemy laws.

Political differences are another source of deep divide in the country. At the time of our visit I was reading Benazir Bhutto's autobiography, entitled *Daughter of Destiny*, which described the events leading to the execution in 1979 of her father, Zulfikar Ali Bhutto, Prime Minister from 1973 to 1977, and her own struggle to become Prime Minister, a position she held from 1988 to 1990 and then again from 1993 to 1996, subsequently being assassinated in December 2007.

Democratic politics has seldom run smoothly in Pakistan, with all politicians being accused, probably justifiably, of corruption and other crimes. Military intervention is a common occurrence, including a coup in 1977 led by General Zia ul-Haq, who ordered the execution of Zulfikar Ali Bhutto, and General Pervez Musharraf, who took power in a bloodless coup in October 1999. Foreign relations with neighbours were also extremely volatile in 1989, with the Afghan war in the process of turning into a civil war following the recent exit of the Russians and the long-running Kashmir dispute with India never being far from boiling over.

I reflected on the impression I had gained from my previous visits to Pakistan in 1971 and 1985 that internal and external politics seemed to be in perpetual turmoil. In 1971, there were not only continuing rumblings over the Kashmir dispute with India, following the second war over the issue six years before, but also the looming civil war over the secession of East Pakistan to become Bangladesh. The creation of East and West Pakistan in 1947 as a single country in two parts divided by 1,000 miles must rank as one of the craziest decisions ever taken in British colonial history.

During my second visit, in 1985, craziness was still in the air, as exemplified by elections that were taking place during a period when political parties were banned. Bemused Pakistani voters were confronted with ballot papers that contained long lists of names, often with multiple entries of common names, such as Mohammed Khan, but with no party affiliation and no further information about the individual's policies. Although the party system in any country is riddled with faults and contradictions, it would be difficult to find a better advert for it than observing the chaos of an election taking place without parties. Not surprisingly, the ban was lifted soon afterwards.

Taking all of the divisive and destabilising factors into account provided me, as the team leader in 1989, with some interesting challenges in terms of organising a nationwide tour for our consultancy project. My company had been commissioned by the Asian Development Bank (ADB) to provide the government of Pakistan (or the Islamic Republic of Pakistan to use the official title) with a national blueprint for increasing exports of fruits and vegetables. It was recognised that there was massive potential to expand exports of such products as onions, citrus, melons and mangoes to markets in the Middle East and Far East. Therefore, we needed to visit all the production areas for horticultural crops, which meant we had to travel to nearly every corner of the country. From the apricot orchards in the Himalayas in the far north, within sight of K2, to the melon fields on the arid, sea level plains near Karachi, there was horticultural production of some description in nearly every location.

I had started to plan our itinerary many months previously. I had the benefit of my previous visits to the country, starting with the 'hippy bus' in 1971, which had travelled from the Indian border near Lahore to the Afghan border beyond Peshawar. Rather more directly relevant to the horticultural subject matter were two trips in 1985 on behalf of a Swiss aid organisation named Intercooperation, which was funding a potato development project, and I had advised them on developing exports to the Gulf States and Malaysia/Singapore. Also, my team had made a short familiarisation visit to Pakistan in June 1989 to liaise with Pakistani contacts in government and the private sector.

The itinerary had to take account of the fact that there were some definite 'no-go' areas. Anywhere near Kashmir was out of the question, and this included some places only a short distance to the east of the capital, Islamabad. All other border areas with India were considered to be sensitive. Also off-limits were the border areas with Afghanistan. Many of the names in this part of the world are wonderfully evocative. The Khyber Pass was definitely well beyond our reach, and I was glad that I had seen this barren, fort-filled landscape in 1971. We were advised that the Federally Administered Tribal Areas close to the Afghan border were best avoided, which was a relief because they already had a frightening reputation long before Mr Osama bin Laden made his assumed hop across from Tora Bora. The main centres of horticultural production in North-West Frontier Province (for inexplicable reasons I love that name) were accessible to us, although we were advised to give the Afghan refugee camps a fairly wide berth.

There was a big debate about whether or not it was safe to visit Quetta and Kalat, in Baluchistan province, not far from the Afghan border. We did go, without encountering any great problems, although there was little sign of the substantial apple orchards that official government statistics suggested should be found there. Perhaps the government statisticians had been less intrepid than us.

Apart from the ethnic, religious and political divisions within the country, we also had to be aware of the dangers posed by criminal gangs. The nature of our project required that we make a lot of visits to rural areas, some of which had a reputation for lawlessness. Our Pakistani hosts always discouraged us from travelling after nightfall in the countryside, but our worst close encounter actually happened in a city. After one rural visit we congratulated ourselves that we had made it back to Karachi just before dusk. Our driver, Abdul, dropped us off at the hotel, but did not turn up at the appointed time the following morning. Eventually we found out why. Only a short distance from the hotel he had stopped at traffic lights, where a small gang of car thieves, attracted by the new four-wheel drive vehicle, had told him to get out of the car. He refused, so they shot him in the head, dumped him at the side of the road and made off with their prize. Miraculously, Abdul survived.

As I write this, I wonder how I would feel if asked to organise a similar consultancy assignment today. Pakistan still suffers from the same ethnic, religious and criminal tensions, but now there are added dimensions. In 1989, I and the other team members recognised that we might get caught up in violence of one kind or another, but we did not expect to be specific targets. Today, as a Westerner, and particularly as a British citizen, I would feel a lot more vulnerable.

Most of our fieldwork took place in Punjab and Sindh provinces where we were largely able to travel around without hindrance, at least in daylight hours. It was surprising to observe the extent to which feudalism still seemed to be alive and well, in spite of land reform legislation, which was widely circumvented. 'Well, what do you expect?' said one of our Pakistani counterparts. 'After all, in spite of the rhetoric, the Bhuttos themselves are a feudal landowning family'. I noticed on some of our farm visits, when we accompanied large landowners, that the poorest workers bent down to touch the hem of the trousers of the 'lord of the manor' in an act of deference that might have been more expected under the caste system in neighbouring India.

Everywhere we were met with great courtesy and friendliness, although, of course, we encountered the typical developing country problems to do with bureaucratic incompetence, poor communications and so on. Occasionally it was the very helpfulness of the people that caused a problem. On a journey from Islamabad to Lahore our car broke down in a place called Gujranwala. The nearly new car, with driver, had been hired for the day so that my colleague and I could visit a couple of farms and markets on the way. As soon as the car ground to a halt a crowd appeared as if from nowhere, as always happens in Pakistan. Gawping curiosity is not a social sin. Once they had overcome their shock at seeing my colleague remove the neck brace he wore for travelling and heard the accompanying sound of Velcro pulling apart, making some of the children think his head was going to fall off, they crowded round the car. As soon as the hapless driver raised the bonnet, the crowd offered various helpful suggestions about the source of the problem, but they did not limit themselves to verbal reasoning. All hands that could reach started pushing and pulling at wires, connectors and other bits of the engine so that the electrics were ruined within a matter of seconds. This was not done in malice but in ignorance and misplaced eagerness to help. Seeing the mayhem under the bonnet I knew that this vehicle was not going to move for many hours, so I made immediate enquiries about finding another car to take us to Lahore. The only possibility was an ancient and battered taxi, which looked like it would have trouble reaching the edge of town but actually achieved the unlikely feat of depositing us at the Avari hotel in Lahore, in a cloud of exhaust smoke, just as the sun went down.

Pakistan is a difficult country to love at the best of times. In comparison to other countries in the Indian sub-continent, such as India and Nepal, or some other countries in the Islamic world, such as Egypt and Jordan, it is a darker and bleaker place, with fewer natural and cultural attractions. That is not to say that Pakistan is entirely lacking in these respects; of course it is not. Pakistan's attractions include sensational mountain scenery in the north; Lahore Fort and other forts in places such as the Khyber Pass (if you could get access to them) and magnificent mosques in all major centres. But if you were a PR officer working for the tourist board you would be fairly hard pressed to make a convincing case for visiting Pakistan in preference to competitor destinations.

Most rural areas are rather barren and few of the cities, with the exception of Lahore, entice you to linger very long. Islamabad, the capital, is a new city with about as much charm as other new capitals. In stark contrast to Islamabad is Rawalpindi, just a few miles up the road, with its teeming hordes and crumbling buildings. Karachi is more modern with some attractive features such as its wide avenues, but it is a vast mass of buildings and people, lacking any real history or identity.

I say all this with a heavy heart because, in many ways, I would like to revisit Pakistan, although I am not entirely sure why. I think the main reason is my memory of the friendliness, courteousness and helpfulness of the people. However, when I try to conjure up other positive recollections, I find that they are overshadowed by darker and more negative images. Some of these might be described as typical of a poor country, such as the hideously crippled and deformed man pushing himself along a Karachi street on a tiny, rickety, wooden trolley, asking passers-by for a few paisa (100 paisa equals 1 rupee). We saw many such heart-rending scenes on our travels.

A worse memory still haunts me to this day. I was travelling in the back of a taxi, casually looking out of the window at the usual chaotic traffic scenes going on around me. Pakistani drivers are serious contenders for the world's worst motorists. They travel at breakneck speed over any terrain that will support a vehicle, regardless of whether it might be the wrong side of the road or off-road or even crossing the road on a pedestrian crossing. Most drivers, in an act of bravado, turn their driving mirrors at a crazy angle away from their line of sight as if to say, 'I'm not one of those wimps who looks in my mirror at the traffic behind'. The motorcyclists are just as bad, often carrying the whole family on a small machine, with Dad driving, a small child or two hanging on at the front and Mum behind Dad enveloped in a *burka* trying to hold on to the smallest child or children. It would be no great surprise to see grandma and grandad bringing up the rear. But this particular horror story does not relate to motorists or motorcyclists but to a single cyclist.

As the taxi pulled up at a traffic light, I noticed a youth jump off the back of a bicycle (most bikes carry two at a time) and then bend down to pick up something. Adjusting my position in the back seat of the taxi to get a better view, I saw that he was gripping the left ankle of a teenage boy lying unconscious in the road and pulling him away from a bike lying on the tarmac. In a flash the first youth jumped back on his bike and his partner pedalled away as the traffic lights changed to green. As my taxi drew away I saw the car battery and the leaking acid for the first time. Presumably the teenager, on some ludicrously dangerous errand, had been resting the battery on the handlebars of his bike and then been hit by a car, leaving him unconscious in the road in an expanding pool of acid. All onlookers had ignored the accident except the youth, who had taken the trouble to drag the comatose figure away from the acid but did not deem it his duty to be involved further. The full realisation of what had happened only hit me as my taxi sped away from the scene. I wanted to help but knew that trying to explain this to my non-English speaking driver would be hopeless. I felt wretched and helpless, which was no use at all to the teenage boy, and I have wondered ever since whether he died or survived, and if so, with what dreadful injuries.

A feeling of helplessness is a common experience when visiting poor countries. Often I can cope with this by adopting the usual international expert's stance of studied detachment or by convincing myself that my very presence in the country on an aid project might just result in some positive benefits to help the people in question. This works on occasion, but one subject where it seldom works for me is in relation to the position of women. I find it difficult to be dispassionate on this subject, even when told by some Muslim women that I should mind my own business, that I do not understand the culture or the religion, and that women themselves are happy with their lot. 'Look, we even have a woman Prime Minister in Pakistan'.

OK, true, but I still can't swallow the argument. The treatment of women in Saudi Arabia, for example, which I have visited several times, including as part of this project as a potential market for Pakistani products, is a case in point. It is inexcusable that women in any country, whether Muslim or non-Muslim, should be denied basic human rights such as the right to vote, to freedom of expression, to work, to move about freely, to marry whom they choose, and to live in safety and without fear of physical harm. Obviously, conditions vary greatly between countries and within different communities and families, but it is hard to ignore this issue when confronted with clear examples of oppression.

The visual manifestation of the downtrodden position of women in some societies is the clothes they wear in public places. If Muslim women choose to wear a simple head covering such as the *hijab* headscarf, then so be it, it's up to them. Even the *chador*, as worn in parts of Iran and Pakistan, at least usually leaves the face uncovered so that women can see where they are going. But I find it difficult to believe that the all-embracing *burka* (much loved by the Taliban, but also common before their time in parts of Afghanistan and Pakistan) is anything other than a sign of subjugation. When looking around at street scenes in the summer months in Rawalpindi or Peshawar, with temperatures over 40 degrees centigrade, it is difficult to believe that any woman would willingly wear a sheet over her entire body, including her head, with a cloth grille to look through, and no arm holes, while trying to carry children and shopping on the back of a motorbike.

It is always amusing on international flights from Saudi Arabia to London, not long after take-off when the plane has reached its cruising altitude, to watch the stream of women walking up the aisle to the toilet, shrouded in head to toe coverings, and then emerging after a few minutes in dresses or jeans and T-shirts, the big smiles on their faces usually mirrored by their male companions. Contrast this with the crazy pantomime on internal flights in Saudi Arabia, which are often delayed taking off while the flight attendants try to accommodate various demands that the black shrouded womenfolk are shifted around so that they are not seated in the same row as unrelated men.

The oppression of women also has significant negative economic effects, particularly when a potentially important part of the workforce is denied the right to work or at least faces limited work opportunities. This became an issue in our study of the potential to develop an efficient horticultural export industry in Pakistan. In packhouses and food processing plants around the world it is very often women who supply much of the labour, partly because they are more dextrous and therefore better suited to this type of work and partly because they are cheaper.

When we were preparing the financial analysis for our project in Pakistan we needed to find out more about whether it was realistic to base our costings on female labour or whether we would have to use less efficient, and more expensive, male labour. As part of our research we visited a Lever Bros date processing factory near to the town of Sukkur in northern Sindh province, on the mighty Indus River, where we were informed that unusually for Pakistan, the great majority of the workforce, numbering many hundreds, were women. After meeting senior company managers (all men of course), who told us that women workers were greatly preferred for general efficiency and for the fiddly tasks involved in preparing dates for sale, we were taken on a tour of inspection of the factory. Prior to entering the main factory building we passed the women's cloakroom where the discarded *burkas*, hanging on hooks, resembled ghosts at a convention. Inside the building was a scene of high productivity, in stark contrast to many similar facilities in Pakistan we had visited, and there was even one solitary wolf whistle as the team of four British visitors passed by. Based on this experience (the efficiency, not the wolf whistle) we felt confident enough to recommend that the employment of women on a large scale was a realistic option for the types of enterprises we were proposing.

As an aside, bearing in mind that multinational companies like Unilever with subsidiaries in developing countries are often accused of exploitation and other dirty tricks, it is fair to point out that this date processing factory in Sukkur was reported by our Pakistani contacts to be a better employer than similar locally owned factories. Not only that, but the date farmers and traders who supplied the factory with its raw material preferred to deal with Lever Bros, because the company paid better prices and was a more reliable business partner. Consumers also favoured the final, packaged product over most local brands. Multinational companies sometimes deserve a bad reputation for their activities in developing countries, but there also many occasions when they are significant and fair contributors to the local economy.

In some ways, the consultancy assignment in Pakistan in 1989 was one of the most difficult of my career, not because of the country or the subject matter but because of the Asian Development Bank (ADB) project officer, who we will call Carl. He and I had rubbed each other up the wrong way since our first meeting at the ADB headquarters in Manila in the Philippines in May 1989. It was ADB's practice at this time, following a tendering process whereby about half a dozen short-listed consultancy companies had submitted their proposals, to call a senior manager from the company that had presented the winning technical bid to Manila to negotiate the financial terms. The euphoria of being told that we had won the first stage of the process was now tempered by the realisation that all would be lost if we could not reach agreement on terms that would provide my company with an adequate level of remuneration.

Unlike most project officers in aid agencies who acted realistically, Carl saw this situation as an opportunity to throw his weight around and make a series of unreasonable demands in the knowledge that the representative of the consultancy company would be very reluctant to go home to the other side of the world with his tail between his legs and report that the contract had been lost because of a failure to agree terms. It did not seem to occur to him that ADB and the consultancy company were on the same side in wanting to produce a successful study that would later be implemented as a successful project. Instead, he seemed more interested in watching the other person squirm as he tried to extract ever more severe concessions over issues such as pay rates and the number of man-days to be worked.

Having completed the negotiations at ADB and started work the following month, I had hoped that our relationship would improve but, instead, it deteriorated. I found him both arrogant and incompetent, an unappealing combination. At one point, in frustration at his slowness to deal with urgent issues, I had mildly complained to him in a fax to Manila. Carl replied with a fax to my Managing Director suggesting that I should be replaced as team leader. In some companies, such a communication from an important client would have been enough for the person in question to be sacked but, fortunately for me, my MD had faith in my ability and insisted that I continue.

Matters continued to get worse for the remainder of the fieldwork phase and only started to improve when he realised that the Pakistanis were delighted with my team's work. Instead of positioning himself to avoid criticism for our expected failure, he now tried to claim some of the credit for our success, although we had succeeded in spite of him. The climax of his turncoat behaviour happened when we returned to Pakistan in February 1990 to present our findings to senior civil servants and businessmen in dissemination seminars held in Islamabad, Karachi and Lahore. His opening remarks on each of these occasions were full of self-congratulation. He remains the only person I have encountered in my working life who I would avoid having a beer with if I met them again.

Earlier in the project Carl had compromised our work in two particular ways. Firstly, he had recruited an unqualified post-harvest specialist, who we will call Fred, who was giving out all sorts of wrong information. Worse still, Fred had a belligerent streak and hated being corrected by the genuine expert, Alan, who was a key member of my team. Accurate post-harvest advice is essential regarding such matters as storage, temperature control, transport and packhouse operations. Pakistan desperately needed good information in this area because existing systems were woefully inadequate, not helped by Fred offering poor or misleading advice.

One of the areas most in need of post-harvest reform was the exporting of mangoes to Dubai and other ports in the Gulf. The mangoes were packed into wooden boxes to the point where each box was over-full; then a wooden lid was hammered down into place, thus crushing the contents. There followed a truck journey of a few hundred miles, in high temperatures, over rough roads, to Karachi port where the boxes were thrown from one man to another until they were roughly stacked in the hold of small boats, known as launches, for the journey to the Gulf.

By the time the cargo was unpacked in Dubai or Abu Dhabi the contents bore a strong resemblance to mango chutney. Not surprisingly the Gulf traders, when interviewed by our team, placed Pakistan in bottom place for the quality of the mangoes that arrived in their wholesale markets, even though the fruit on the tree was among the best. Correct post–harvest handling advice, if adopted by the exporters, could transform prospects in this area because Pakistan was a relatively nearby supplier with an excellent product at source. There is no excuse for aid agencies employing unqualified 'experts', such as Fred, who was offering erroneous advice and had no report writing skills.

The perceptive reader at this juncture might point out that I admitted in an earlier chapter to being a sham as an international 'expert' and, therefore, I might be guilty of being the pot that calls the kettle black. There is some truth in this, but in my own defence I would point out that, unlike Fred, I knew my own limitations and always bowed to others with superior knowledge. I had also worked hard at developing my understanding of the agri-food sector. In addition to practical experience I had done a number of courses and I could now pass myself off, quite realistically, as an agricultural marketing specialist and agricultural economist.

Furthermore, an option for the person lacking detailed specialist knowledge is to become the leader if one has the skills required. Being a team leader played to my strengths and hid my weaknesses. I was good at building a team of specialists and getting them to work as a team. I was happy to deal with the aid agencies, local ministries and other official contacts, often in interminable meetings, while the team members got on with their practical fieldwork. I was reasonably good at seeing the broader picture and persuading the team members to pull in the same direction rather than getting bogged down in their own little areas of specialisation. I could also present the findings in a coherent report, which is more than can be said of many consultants. My shortcomings were that I never developed the level of technical knowledge about 'growing things' and 'processing things' that I really should have done, but this could be camouflaged if I surrounded myself with experts like Alan.

The second way in which Carl presented us with unnecessary problems was by giving us an unrealistically hurried timetable for carrying out the visits to overseas markets. The terms of reference required us to research the market prospects for Pakistan in selected southeast Asian countries and nearby Gulf markets. This was grist to the mill for me, because I had extensive experience of such work and enjoyed visiting importers and wholesale markets to collect the necessary information.

In fact, I had carried out an almost identical exercise in 1985 as part of the potato marketing study, which afforded both good and bad memories. The good memories related to a trip to Kuala Lumpur and Singapore in the company of my counterpart officer, named Iqbal, who was a manager in one of Pakistan's government-owned food marketing companies. We probably made an odd couple in the teeming wholesale markets where Chinese traders conducted all their business, whether over the phone or face-to-face, at a very high level of decibels. Iqbal dressed in traditional Pakistani garb, with henna-dyed hair to indicate that he had made a Hajj to Mecca and a tall, gangly Englishman towering over the throng, clutching his briefcase. Our work schedule had to be arranged carefully so that Iqbal could fulfil his prayer commitments, and our eating places had to be rigorously checked to avoid any possibility of infringing Muslim rules, but we worked well together and became good friends.

The bad experience in 1985 took place in Saudi Arabia. I had parted company from Iqbal in Singapore and headed for Riyadh to meet up with a colleague who had already been there for a few days and was ensconced in the Al Batha hotel. My colleague was renowned for trying to save every penny he could from the daily allowances, so it was no great surprise to find that the Al Batha was a rather downbeat place compared to usual Saudi standards. This negative first impression was reinforced by a telephone call received shortly after checking in. As a seasoned international traveller I found it no great surprise to pick up the receiver and hear a voice say, 'I am coming to your room to f*** you'. What made this call different, and made my blood run cold, was that the caller was male and the Saudi-accented voice was very menacing. 'Oh no you're not' I squeaked, with a combination of righteous indignation and real fear.

I found this experience extremely intimidating, not least because of recalling travellers' tales, whether true or false, about instances of male rape in this part of the world and hearing reports that in any situation where it is a case of a foreigner's word against a Saudi national, the police or courts will always take the side of the local person. To make matters worse, each time I entered my hotel room the telephone rang as soon as I shut the door, clearly indicating that I was being watched. There followed the usual heavy breathing and the familiar refrain repeated over and over again. Complaints to the hotel management made no difference and, after a sleepless night spent checking the door and window locks every few minutes, it was with enormous relief that I checked out of the hotel the following day and fled to the airport.

The travel schedule in July 1989 included six export markets – Malaysia, Singapore, Hong Kong, Kuwait, the United Arab Emirates (UAE) and Saudi Arabia – and Carl, in his wisdom, had specified that the work must be completed in a very short space of time. This presented us with a particular problem in Saudi Arabia, because the only way we could get the work done in time was to visit at the time of the Hajj when millions of pilgrims were arriving in the Kingdom.

I was already slightly behind schedule as a result of being detained on arrival at the airport in Kuwait for a number of hours, part of the time in a non-air conditioned room with the temperature gauge showing 47 degrees centigrade, because my visa obtained from the Kuwaiti representative in Karachi was invalid. Just one of the hiccups of this kind of work.

On arrival in Riyadh, I rendezvoused with my colleague Chris, who had arrived a little before me and was under strict instructions not to stay at the Al Batha hotel. We knew that the Hajj should be avoided at all costs because air transport was disrupted by the arrival of a few million pilgrims and normal business activity was largely put on hold, but Carl's schedule was set in stone, so we had to persevere. Chris and I spent quite a lot of time at various airports waiting for planes that were running many hours late as a result of unscheduled trips to pick up more pilgrims, while watching the hordes of people, many dressed in simple pilgrim's robes, making their way towards Mecca. To make matters worse and the delays longer, reports came through on the 9th July that two bombs had exploded in Mecca; the Saudis blamed Shia extremists, and some time later 16 Kuwaitis were beheaded for the crime.

Not surprisingly, Jeddah was the most congested of all and it was difficult to make progress with our business visits, but I did have the consolation of meeting a certain Mr M. Ali, former heavyweight champion of the world, in a lift at our hotel. My mother had died a few months previously after many years of struggle against the effects of Parkinson's disease, and it was sad to see this supreme athlete obviously suffering the early stages of the same illness.

After overcoming all difficulties, my team combined our findings from the fieldwork stage in Pakistan, together with the results of the market studies, which revealed that Pakistani exporters currently had a very poor reputation in all export markets, and identified real opportunities for improvement and success. If our proposals were followed there were excellent prospects in many sectors including kinnow (a high-yield mandarin hybrid) and other citrus exports from Punjab, mango exports from Sindh and onion and garlic exports from multiple locations.

The good news, in the end, was that the export strategy blueprint was very well received by the government of Pakistan, and it was reported to me over the following years, on a number of occasions, that several Pakistani export businesses successfully implemented our recommendations.

CHAPTER 12

RUSSIA, 1991 AND 1992

'This is not Africa' said Evgeny politely, but with a definite edge to his voice. I looked up from my soup and was about to tell him that I had an A level in Geography and was very well aware that we were not in Africa when I realised what he meant. Like most international experts working on aid projects I had spent the majority of my career working in developing countries, particularly in Africa, and like most Africa bores I tended to start a lot of sentences with 'When I was in Africa...'. But now I was working in Russia and the proud Russians did not like their country to be equated with the Third World.

In the early 1990s a complete transformation took place in the activities of aid agencies and the international experts who worked on their projects. The collapse of the Berlin Wall in 1989 signalled the end of the Cold War. Aid agencies which had previously only operated in Africa, Asia and Latin America, now had to cope with an entirely new set of demands in the former eastern bloc. Western governments, particularly those in the European Union, were scared stiff that law and order would break down in the east and that hordes of migrants would set off for the west in their Trabants and Ladas. The solution, it was argued, was to pump lots of aid funds into the east to assist with economic development and political stability.

Looking back, nearly 30 years on, it seems incredible to remember that Western countries mounted enormous programmes of both bilateral and multilateral aid for Russia and the other 14 countries that had constituted the USSR. The European Union created the TACIS programme in 1991 (Technical Assistance to the Commonwealth of Independent States). The British aid programme created a new organisation, the Know-How Fund, to offer aid to Eastern Europe and was later expanded eastwards. An entirely new organisation, the European Bank for Reconstruction and Development (EBRD), headquartered in London, was launched in 1991 as a multilateral investment bank to promote market economies in former communist countries. Many more aid agencies were struggling in chaotic times to operate in totally new environments.

This was a bonanza time for the consultancy companies that carry out most of the planning and implementation work for the aid agencies. It started with lots of work in places such as Poland and Hungary. Then the realisation dawned that the Soviet Union itself was about to fall apart. Many 'wise after the event' people claimed that they had seen this coming, but they hadn't really, it took everyone by surprise, including the Russians. The scale of the problem for the aid agencies was instantly magnified. Sorting out Poland and Hungary suddenly seemed easy. Now there was a vast empire to reform, which was economically backward and where all sorts of Dr No-type characters were about to get their hands on nuclear weapons. Horror stories abounded of Soviet nuclear scientists, who had not received their salaries for several months, selling missile technology to the highest bidders, including North Korea. Moreover, Chernobyl was a recent memory and any number of other power stations were in danger of providing the ultimate fireworks display. The answer, it seemed, was to pump loads more aid funds into the region. Every sector of the Russian economy – energy, food, banking and all the others – had funds allocated for projects to help in the transformation from failing command system to the bright new dawn of a western style market economy.

The Western consultancy companies, whose services were needed to design and implement these projects, could not believe their luck. For those that were able to adapt quickly, there was suddenly an avalanche of work. The only problem was that all the people involved, both those working directly for the aid agencies and those working for the contractors, had experience largely gained in the Third World. So we all had to reinvent ourselves very swiftly.

It was June 1992 and Evgeny and I were sitting in the restaurant of the Hotel Volga in Samara (formerly known as Kuybyshev in Soviet times), a city on the Volga River about 650 miles east of Moscow. Evgeny was working as my guide and interpreter. After a great deal of endeavour he had managed to get us something to eat. Almost immediately on our arrival at the hotel a few days earlier he had set about establishing our food supply. This was not a simple matter of going to the restaurant, looking at the menu and ordering any dish that took your fancy. Oh no, how naïve can you be? It's true that you would have been shown a menu, with long lists of food to satisfy any tastes, but each time an attempt was made to place an order, an uninterested waiter would reply that it was not available. Tiring of this little game, you would then ask the waiter 'Well what do you have?' to which he would reply triumphantly, 'nothing'. These were dire times in Russia, annoying for a visiting 'expert' but totally disastrous for most of the local population.

Aware of the need for a more cunning approach, Evgeny had immediately set about identifying the person responsible for food procurement for the hotel kitchens. This turned out to be a stout, sour-faced woman of about fifty, who bore a strong resemblance to Nikita Khrushchev in a dress. Evgeny proceeded to ingratiate himself with this harridan by offering all sorts of unlikely compliments about her beauty and, more importantly, plying her with gifts of chocolate. To my astonishment, he had insisted on stocking up with half a suitcase load of chocolate prior to our departure from Moscow on the 18-hour train journey to Samara, and now I saw the wisdom of his ways.

The only other people eating in the restaurant had an alternative approach to securing their food supply. These gentlemen were distinguished by their sharp suits and sunglasses. In fact, I never saw them without sunglasses even in the dimly lit hotel bar in the small hours of the morning. They must have been in great danger of falling down the hotel's unlit stairs (nobody had replaced the bulbs) or dropping into the many holes in the street with manhole covers missing. But they were slaves to fashion and the sunglasses were part of their uniform. As Evgeny informed me, these gentlemen were mafia. Some were Chechens and some were Georgians, up from the southern republics on goodness knows what business. Even their vehicles had sunglasses. These were usually flashy Japanese four-wheel drive monsters with the windows blacked out. For some reason when these customers entered the restaurant, the waiters suddenly became interested and the best dishes of the house rapidly materialised.

Although this was my fourth visit to what was now called the Former Soviet Union (FSU), I was still struggling to understand my surroundings. This was a very strange place indeed. Before my first visit to Russia in November 1991, still the USSR then, I thought I knew what to expect. I had avidly kept up with the news about Mr Gorbachev and his signature policies of *perestroika* and *glasnost*. I had read most of the books by Alexander Solzhenitsyn and even a few of the classics by Dostoyevsky, Tolstoy and those other great men with long beards. I had even done a course on the Russian political system as part of my degree many years before. To cap it all, *Doctor Zhivago* was my favourite film. But nothing had prepared me for my first visit.

It did not start well. We were a group of about a dozen people representing a collection of companies known as the British Food Consortium (BFC), paid by British government aid funds to go to Russia to seek out opportunities, with local organisations, to improve the food supply. Our group included experts in the various food sectors – meat, dairy, sugar beet and so on. My responsibility was the fruit and vegetable sector, including processed products such as fruit juices. I needed an engineer to accompany me who was well acquainted with factory techniques. I had recruited a guy called Dan for this purpose. We were all due to meet at Terminal 1, Heathrow Airport on November 4th 1991 at 8:30 am. All were there at the appointed time with the exception of Dan.

We were an odd-looking lot. Aware of the temperatures to be faced in Russia in November, we had taken elaborate precautions. I had borrowed an ill-fitting sheepskin coat from a friend and an ill-fitting Russian fur hat from someone in my village who had worked at the British embassy in Moscow many years previously. Chic I was not, nor were most of my colleagues, but I intended to keep as warm as possible. Dan arrived just in time to catch the flight, looking flustered because his taxi had got stuck in traffic. He seemed surprised that the M4, the busiest stretch of motorway in Europe, should have impeded his progress to the airport during the rush hour on a Monday morning. Worse was to follow. Dan had carefully placed his overcoat on the kitchen table ready to pick up when the taxi arrived, but the strain of remembering to pick up his suitcase, briefcase and coat was too much and the coat was forgotten. Dan seemed unconcerned about the prospect of facing a Russian winter with nothing warmer than a Marks and Spencer's suit. 'I may have to wear a vest,' he said brightly.

Moscow's Sheremetyevo Airport in 1991 was an unwelcoming place. Queuing was a national pastime in Russia at this time. Bakeries and other food shops that actually had anything to sell immediately attracted queues, and just to get you into the habit you started queuing at the airport. Admittedly this was not as bad as the five hours I once spent queuing to get a passport stamp at Kiev airport, but it was bad enough. When you eventually reached passport control you had to stand in a strange little booth with mirrors above your head (was there a politburo decree that toupees were not allowed?) while a gruff official scrutinised every minute detail of your visa and then reluctantly allowed you to pass through. After a protracted search for your luggage, followed by more layers of bureaucracy to prove that the luggage was actually yours, you passed through to the arrivals hall. Somebody in the politburo had had the bright idea of making the ceilings in many parts of the airport very low and covered with what looked like dark circular copper plates. This had the depressing effect of lowering the ceilings to the extent that it appeared that a great weight was resting on your head. Light and airy it was not. Never mind, the main thing after a long flight and arrival in a strange airport is to be met by someone with a welcoming smile. Thankfully our hosts from Kamenka town in Penza Oblast (region), with interpreters, were there to meet us, with big smiles.

We were driven into Moscow, straight to a nightclub. 'Blimey, this is a bit different' I thought. We were treated to some erotic, but tasteful, dancing and a good meal, washed down with lashings of vodka and *champanska* (the Russian version of champagne). This was a lot of fun and all seemed well with the world.

In fact it would have been if this experience had been followed by a good night's sleep in a comfortable bed. But you soon learn that Russia is a land of contrasts. Immediately after the meal we were poured on to a bus and embarked on a long and highly uncomfortable 400-mile journey through the night. This was my first glimpse of the country, and pretty dismal it looked as we headed south-east from the capital. The thousands of almost identical tower blocks on the outskirts of Moscow gave way to a vast expanse of darkness and emptiness with occasional shadowy figures going about their business. At irregular intervals, truck drivers were visible at the side of the road lighting fires under their ancient vehicles to heat up the diesel sufficiently to get started. Our own attempts to buy diesel in the small towns along the way proved fruitless. Russia might be one of the main oil producers in the world, but that did not mean that you could easily buy a tank full of fuel when you wanted it. Eventually a reluctant petrol station worker parted with enough diesel for us to make it to Kamenka and we arrived in time for a late breakfast.

We were being housed in what the Russians call a sanatorium, in a forest on the outskirts of town. The prime use of such places was to give the heroes of Soviet labour a few days' rest and recuperation, in Butlin-style holiday camp surroundings, as a reward for a lifetime of toil in some factory or other place of work. We sat down to a breakfast consisting of three or four courses, none of which were identifiable and all of which were inedible. Politeness to our hosts required that we smile a lot and offer the unlikely explanation that we were still full from our meal in the nightclub twelve hours before.

We proceeded upstairs to our bedrooms. Each unit consisted of two bedrooms with a shared bathroom. The bedrooms were basic but quite comfortable. The only problem, one I learned to expect throughout my travels in the FSU, was the length of the bed. Someone in the politburo had decreed that a standard bed length should be about 5ft 10ins. This was fine for all those people of 5ft 9ins or less but for those of us who are 6ft 2ins, it creates a problem. This is exacerbated by the further requirement, no doubt reinforced by a politburo edict, that all beds should have a headboard and a footboard. I learned to carry a tool set with me so that I could dismantle the footboards, and there are dozens of such useless pieces of wood hidden under beds throughout the FSU. You also quickly learn to carry a bathroom plug with you on your travels because only the most Westernised hotels are equipped with this luxury; the Russians preferring to wash in running water rather than in water containing their own filth, you have to admit they have a point.

It was the shared bathroom located between the bedrooms occupied by Dan and myself that provided the most surprises. The plumbing looked like an exhibit at the Tate Modern assembled by drunken chimpanzees. There were pipes everywhere, sticking out of walls at crazy angles and crossing the room at below head height so that you had to duck to get under them. If you turned on a tap the whole room started vibrating loudly and, after an interval of a minute or two, a foul smelling brown liquid suddenly shot out with great force just at the point when you had given up waiting. The hot water tap always gave forth cold water. The cold water tap, on occasion, gave a burst of hot water, but sod's law determined that this never happened when you wanted to take a shower. The whole thing was an affront to Dan's engineering skills and, with a sense of foreboding, we began to realise what lay in store for us when we started our tour of the food factories.

Over the following days, as we visited state farms and factories, the theme of Russia as a land of contrasts was never far from our minds. The land of space travel and high culture was also the land of poverty and decay. I shuddered to think that in my student days in the 1960s I had toyed with Marxist sympathies, before quickly rejecting them. We were witnessing a system, the command system, in the final stages of collapse. The food supply chain illustrated the problem. Previously Moscow had determined what was produced on all the state farms, where it was stored or processed, which state-owned shops the food should be delivered to and at what price it should be sold. Wonderful in theory, but incompetence and inefficiency were inevitable consequences of such a centralised system. Between the seed going into the ground and the consumer buying the product, there were thousands of workers and bureaucrats, none of whom had any incentive to do their jobs well. They just tried to keep out of trouble and do the minimum possible to get by. The state farms, using low-quality inputs and equipment, produced low-quality food. 'Rubbish in and rubbish out' could easily have been the motto of the storage centres, processing plants and shops further down the food chain. The downtrodden Russian consumer was left to sift through the dross.

The state farms provided the greatest shock. They were enormous, often covering thousands of hectares. The state farm workers, or peasants as they were universally called, lived in villages of simple single-storey houses with minimal facilities. Some had no electricity and some even had no running water. Imagine living in a village located on the vast open snow-covered plains of Russia and going out to a standpipe with a bucket to collect your water. This may be a common scene in parts of Africa and other places, but not in these temperatures. You wondered how the peasants came to live here in the first place. Were they left over from the old pre-1918 aristocratic estates? Had they been forcibly sent here in one of Stalin's purges? Surely their forefathers had not come here voluntarily. It's not surprising that many peasants' idea of heaven is to move to a cockroach-infested apartment in a town or city where at least there would be electricity, heating, and not only running water but hot water.

After a day's work of minimum effort as a tractor driver or some other job, the average peasant would rush home to start some serious work on his or her small private plot of land. Each peasant family was allowed a set area of land to keep a few animals and grow crops for their own consumption or for sale in the licensed, private markets in the towns. Such aberrations were tolerated by the communist system in order to allow at least some reasonable quality food into the urban areas. The peasants' patches of land provided an oasis of efficient cultivation on the state farms and the private markets provided an oasis of higher quality produce in the urban areas, but only for those who could pay the prices. The more entrepreneurial peasants might even afford a motorbike and sidecar from these earnings to replace the horse and cart which was the more usual form of peasant transport around the villages.

Amid this disintegrating system there were some state farm directors (roughly equivalent to a lord of the manor in medieval Britain, except that they did not own the land), who were trying to introduce innovations to bring in some extra money. You could tell the 'old school' directors by whether or not they still had a picture of Lenin adorning the wall of their offices. But the new breed directors were more prepared to exploit the opportunities thrown up by the removal of restrictions placed on running the farm as a business. A few of these schemes were well founded, but many more were pathetically ill-judged projects set up by people who had no previous concept of satisfying consumer demand. The idea that you produced what people actually wanted to buy was an alien concept. It would take some time for the supply-led approach to change to a demand-led mentality.

On another visit to Russia, a state farm director asked me if I would like to see the newly installed juice-making facility that he hoped would transform the failing finances of his farm. He proudly took me to a well-constructed small building containing some gleaming new machinery. I asked what type of juice he intended to produce, expecting the reply, 'apple', but to my surprise he answered, 'cabbage'. 'Is there a big demand for cabbage juice in this area?' I asked. The director looked at me vacantly. Beginning to flounder, I persevered, 'But why produce cabbage juice?' He looked at me as if I was an idiot. 'Because we've got a lot of cabbages' came the reply.

The food factories were no better. Most existed in a no-man's-land between state-ownership and privatisation. In other words, the old system of guaranteed supply of raw materials and guaranteed sales to state shops had broken down but had not yet been replaced by any meaningful alternative. The best factories were snapped up by the emerging breed of Russian entrepreneurs, but the majority of factories were drifting aimlessly along with proposals being prepared for various forms of workers' ownership. But would you want a share of a rusting hulk of a factory, with antiquated equipment and no likely market for its revolting products? Apart from juices, most of the factories were producing various forms of preserved fruit and vegetables sold in glass jars. Canning was not widely used in Russia because, as Dan explained, it's much easier to poison large numbers of people if the canning process goes wrong but bottling is relatively harmless. The Russians trusted themselves to build nuclear reactors but not to produce canned tomatoes.

Even the glass jars were not without problems. There was a perennial national shortage of one-litre jars, reportedly as part of Mr Gorbachev's anti-alcoholism campaign because they were re-used for alcoholic drinks, so the factories mostly used enormous three-litre jars. These products were not user-friendly. The sight of little old ladies struggling to carry one of these monsters home from the shops was not easily forgotten.

It was the shops that provided the best hope for a quick breakthrough to a market-based system. Although the state shops we visited in 1991 and 1992 were in a bad state of disorganisation and disrepair, with long rows of empty shelves, it was clear that the potential existed for them to be transformed with just a bit of business flair and imagination. Shops are much easier to privatise than factories or farms, but there were also hazards in this process, because as soon as the newly privatised shops showed signs of making some money those nice men in their sharp suits and sunglasses would pay a visit just to make sure that you were properly protected.

One of the first things for the shops to change was the crazy purchasing system. Typically, a customer, after queuing outside, would then have to follow a convoluted series of tasks to purchase even one simple item. Firstly, she would fight her way to the appropriate counter and ask to be shown the item of interest, which would always be kept out of reach. Having decided to purchase the item, she would be given a chitty to take to the cashier's desk, which would probably be some distance away in another part of the shop. Inevitably, there would be a long queue there. Sometimes fault would be found with some detail of the chitty which would require a return visit to the counter. Eventually payment would be made and a receipt given for the customer to take back to the counter where, after another fight for position, the receipt would be handed in and the product passed over the counter, if it had not been sold, lost or gone bad in the intervening time. How the sadists in the politburo must have laughed on the day they devised this system.

As Dan and I, together with others from the BFC team, proceeded on a bus tour of the region's farms, factories and shops it became increasingly obvious that Dan's strategy of adding a vest to his attire was not going to do the trick of withstanding the

Russian winter. He was gradually turning bluer and bluer. Our hosts from the local administration had simply been amused by his appearance as we left the sanatorium in the morning, perhaps thinking that he was equipped with some cunningly clever form of thermal underwear. But as his colour changed from mauve to blue and he started coughing in a most alarming way, their concern mounted. It was not going to look good if a member of one of the first groups of international experts to visit this particular region died of exposure on the first day. So at the next factory they borrowed a blue worker's coat and an old fur hat. They also insisted that the nurse at the sanatorium should give Dan a chest rub on our return.

This suggestion was met with some alarm by Dan, who had images of some of the burly ladies we had met in the farms and factories giving him a working over, but in the event he became the object of all our envy. The nurse turned out to be young, blonde, attractive and dressed in one of those feminine uniforms that British nurses used to wear before they were replaced by the modern version of shapeless functionality. Dan emerged from the treatment room with an enormous smile on his face but also coughing just enough to ensure that a return visit the following day would be necessary. In fact, that cough turned out to be surprisingly difficult to cure, requiring treatment on every day until our departure, and then it miraculously disappeared on the journey back to Moscow. Several other members of the BFC team developed a staggering array of ailments affecting various parts of their anatomies, which they claimed warranted visits to the treatment room, but all were dismissed with a polite smile. Only Dan made it to the inner sanctum.

Before visiting Russia, I shared the popular misconception

that Russian women are unattractive. Perhaps television images of Russian women shot-putters and discus throwers at the Olympics had influenced me. But not all young Russian women look like Tamara Press, who mysteriously disappeared from the international athletics scene when sex testing was introduced. In fact, very few of them do. Most young Russian women are slim, feminine and well dressed. They take great pains over their appearance. Walking down a city street in Russia is like witnessing a fashion parade. Even the girls from the state farms, when they go into town or to a social event, look like they are dressed for a wedding. When seeing a couple of girls from a state farm village, dressed in high heels and short skirts, trying to negotiate their way along a dirt road covered in snow or mud, you have to admire their dedication and determination. But something seems to happen to most Russian women around the age of 35; they become twice or three times the size they were a few years previously. This is not down to multiple childbirths, because nearly every Russian woman has only one child, partly a function of cramped living conditions, but something else happens and the slim, young beauty is transformed into a larger version of herself.

When they get older still, perhaps reaching grandmother age, Russian women become known as *babushkas*. The stereotypical *babushka* wears a woollen headscarf pulled tightly down over her ears and a dowdy brown coat and bends forward into the wind carrying heavy shopping. It was the lives of these old ladies that I found the most shocking during my early visits to Russia. Life had always been hard but the breakdown of the old system and the erosion of pension values by rampant inflation meant that many were tipped over the boundary from just surviving to desperate poverty.

It was a common sight to see lines of *babushkas* standing in the street in sub-zero temperatures selling one or two pathetic items of second-hand clothing or kitchen implements from their own homes. One freezing old lady affected me so much that I bought her entire stock of three small geranium plants, and paid a large premium over her asking price, on condition that she went home and sat in front of the fire. Some old women were driven to do hard manual labour such as road sweeping or loading snow on to a lorry with a spade to clear the pavements. Perhaps the most pathetic sight I saw during the first trip was a frail *babushka* from a state farm village where the water supply had failed, taking a bucket to a nearby lake where she first had to break the ice before filling the bucket with unclean water and then staggering back to her hovel. This sight was the more poignant because we were on our way at the time to visit the poet Lermontov's birthplace in a fine country house near Kamenka, as part of our hosts' proud wish for us to appreciate their country's rich cultural heritage.

Dan was having trouble being taken seriously during our visits to the food factories. With his borrowed clothes he looked like the man who does the sweeping up rather than an engineer of international experience. So we decided to make a detour to a department store to buy him a coat. This was the worst time for Russian shops and, therefore, Russian consumers. It was the intermediate period between the end of state ownership, with goods supplied from state factories, and private ownership, with goods supplied from many sources, mostly abroad. In a fairly short time the empty shelves would be overflowing with Levi jeans, Gucci handbags (probably fake) and all manner of other imported consumer goods for those who could afford them, but on this day the place was like a morgue. The shoe department was the most pathetic. The long rows of empty shelves contained just one shoe, not a pair, but a single shoe. Perhaps an amputee from the conflict in Afghanistan had taken the other one. The outerwear department was slightly better stocked and Dan purchased a rather fine woollen coat that we thought was cheap, but our Russian colleagues pointed out that the price was equivalent to a month's wages for an average worker.

The saving grace of Russia during those early visits was the hospitality of the people. Without that I would cheerfully have never visited the place again. As well as being regularly invited to people's homes, there was also a lot of hospitality in the form of banquets in those early days of 1991 and 1992 when visiting teams of international experts still had a novelty value. In a couple of years' time, foreign visitors were two a penny and attracted no special attention, but in the early 90s, outside Moscow and St. Petersburg, Westerners still had a rarity value, particularly in areas which had previously been restricted zones. In June 1992 I was a member of another British Food Consortium team, this time visiting Nizhny Novgorod, which had been a closed city in Soviet times. In those days it had been called Gorky and had not only been a military city but also a place of internal exile for such celebrated dissidents as Andrei Sakharov and his wife, Yelena Bonner. We were among the early Westerners to visit the newly reopened city, and were treated like Hollywood stars.

The Governor of Nizhny Novgorod Oblast (region) at the time was a very young and impressive Boris Nemtsov, a scientist turned reform-minded politician with a keen interest in market economics. This, combined with his wish to practise speaking

English, meant that he met our team on a number of occasions. His reputation spread and the following year, 1993, Margaret Thatcher paid him and his city a visit. His star shone brightly under Boris Yeltsin, culminating in a brief period as Deputy Prime Minister in 1998, but he later became an outspoken critic of the corruption under Vladimir Putin and was brutally assassinated within sight of the Kremlin in Moscow on 27th February 2015.

The Russians love a formal dinner or a banquet. It's an excuse to consume better food than is normally available along with vast quantities of alcohol, usually in the form of vodka, *champanska* and brandy. There are very serious social consequences resulting from the Russian obsession with alcohol, but it does make for a lively party. You soon learn to keep your vodka glass full with mineral water in the hope that your hosts will be dissuaded from refilling it for the umpteenth time, but it seldom fools them. You learn to say '*chut-chut* '(just a little) in the vain hope that the glass will not be filled to the brim. You also try and resist their entreaties to throw the vodka down your throat in one gulp, '*dobna*' (down in one). The purpose of drinking is to get drunk, and you get drunk quicker by drinking fast. Sipping is an alien concept and teetotalism is totally incomprehensible to them.

Toasts form an important part of these occasions, no matter whether you are in a private apartment or being entertained by the local civic dignitaries. It is expected that the guests will respond to the toasts, and if things are really going with a swing then just about everyone round the table will propose a toast at some point in the evening. Therefore, you quickly learn to have some appropriate words at the ready, otherwise you risk standing up, having had far too much to drink, and mumbling incoherently. To make matters worse, it is greatly appreciated if you deliver your toast in Russian rather than having it translated by one of the interpreters. With typical British lack of facility for languages, this was usually done badly, but the Russians would smile benevolently as their language was unmercifully mangled. We tried to learn a few key words for such occasions – *druzhba* (friendship) and *genshina* (women) always went down well. The real challenge arose if your pet subjects had already been used in previous toasts. Faced with this dilemma on one occasion, and with my brain addled by vodka, the only Russian words that came into my head were the names of various vegetables and our mystified hosts found themselves toasting cabbage, beetroot, cucumbers and tomatoes.

Even more embarrassing were the times when it was necessary to sing a song or do a turn of some kind. It's not uncommon for Russians around the dinner table to break into song, perhaps a Russian folk song, or play an instrument, usually very well, and then turn expectantly to their guests to respond. At such times I always greatly regretted that my piano playing had never progressed beyond a one-handed, half-tempo rendering of 'Home on The Range'. The only alternative was to sing a song, but that presented the problem of remembering the words. I often made a mental note to learn the lyrics of at least one British folk song or Ralph McTell's 'Streets of London', but I never did.

The fearsome Ludmila looked over at Peter Street and me and told us that it was our turn to sing something from England. Peter was last heard of in this book in Afghanistan in 1978. He and I worked together at intervals over a period of more than 20 years, originally for the same institute and then as fellow directors of a private consultancy company. We were in Samara, about a year after my first visit with Evgeny, to organise the start-up of a two-year European Union funded project in the nearby town of Togliatti, famous as the home of the much-derided Lada car.

Ludmilla and her cronies, who it later transpired were probably ex-KGB officers looking for a new income stream, were trying to muscle in on all the aid projects starting in the region. She was giving a dinner party for us and Fritz from a rival German consultancy company. She was petite, beautiful and strangely frightening. When she said 'Sing', you sang. I looked over at Peter, and this former Professor of Agriculture at Reading University and usually self-assured individual was a gibbering wreck. 'You lead and I'll follow,' he said unhelpfully. I made a determined effort to stop quivering and concentrate on the task in hand but my mind was a blank. Playing for time, I challenged Fritz to give a rendering of Beethoven's *Ode to Joy*. A rather self-satisfied look came over his face and he started off '*Freude, schoener Goetterfunken...*' and I must admit the clever sod gave a very good impromptu performance. This only added to the pressure on Peter and myself. 'You lead and I'll follow', was all that Peter had to offer. Goodness knows why it came into my head, but we ended up singing 'I'm forever blowing bubbles' – at least I sang and Peter opened and closed his mouth noiselessly. I gave a rather implausible explanation about it being the theme tune of one of London's football clubs and therefore almost a folk song. I imagine this experience left our ex-KGB hosts wondering how on earth the USSR lost the Cold War.

Why are the British so bad at these things? Is it British reserve, or are we just bad performers? The collective embarrassment was greatest at a large civic function to welcome the BFC team. The evening started off with lovely young Russian ladies, dressed in national costume, performing the traditional Russian greeting ceremony of offering bread. This was followed by several local musicians and a school choir giving faultless performances of works by various Russian composers. Then, horror of horrors, it became clear that we were expected to respond. Presumably they thought that out of a group of about a dozen people at least one or two would be able to play something by Elgar or Vaughan Williams. But no, embarrassed looks all round, a quick whispered conference resulted in a combined rendering of:

The Grand old Duke of York, he had 10,000 men,
He marched them up to the top of the hill and he marched them down again.
When they were up they were up and when they were down they were down.
And when they were only half way up they were neither up nor down.

This produced polite but bewildered applause from our hosts. They had given us Tchaikovsky, Borodin and Rimsky Korsakov, and in return we had given them a nursery rhyme about men walking up and down a hill.

Russian hospitality is matched only by Russian generosity in the form of giving gifts. Especially in the early days, we always returned home laden with presents. Regular gifts were bottles of Stolichnaya vodka, those black and gold painted wooden bowls and spoons that you see everywhere in Russia or Matryoshka dolls (my favourite had Yeltsin on the outside, then Brezhnev, then Khrushchev and little Joe Stalin in the middle). Some gifts were more unusual than others. I still have a piece of green pottery with many interlocking components that I was given by one state farm director. Finding the right words to express your immense gratitude for something whose purpose is totally unknown to you is quite tricky.

Most generous of all was Nina. Her husband was a middle-ranking official at one of the storage centres in Kamenka, and he absolutely insisted on inviting us all back to his apartment for lunch. Nina had about 30 minutes of warning that a party of 10 complete strangers was going to descend upon her small one-bedroom apartment for a meal, but instead of going berserk, which my wife would quite justifiably have done in similar circumstances, she kept thanking us for doing her and her family the honour of eating at their home. In fact, in the event, she got about 40 minutes of warning, because the lift got stuck between floors on the way up to the eighth floor. This was apparently common practice, and, on closer inspection, it seemed to be a minor miracle that the lift ever got off the ground at all.

This was our first experience of Russian home living. In any Russian town or city it is quite rare to find houses. Instead there are endless rows of almost identical tower blocks containing almost identical one and two-bedroom apartments. There is a Russian joke about a man getting off a train at the wrong station, catching a bus to the wrong tower block, entering the wrong apartment and only noticing his mistake when he gets into bed with the wrong wife.

Although the communal areas of the tower blocks tend to be dirty and foul smelling, the flats themselves are usually tidy and stuffed full of furniture, and they provide object lessons in the efficient usage of space. Heating and hot water are provided on a communal basis, which is great so long as the local power station is working, but everyone is cut off together if not. The radiators in the apartments usually have no means of temperature control, which is why it is a common sight to see tower blocks with lots of windows open when the outside temperature is 20 degrees below freezing.

I think Nina probably emptied the larders of just about every apartment in the tower block. She served a wonderful meal, of course washed down with gallons of vodka, accompanied by any number of toasts to our everlasting friendship. The idea that this group of people could so easily have been enemies on opposite sides of a nuclear war, if recent history had taken a slightly different course, seemed utterly ridiculous. The afternoon passed very pleasantly without a stroke of work being done, which made the BFC team members feel guilty, but our hosts consoled us by saying that we were engaged in the much more important task of international reconciliation. It was as good an excuse as any.

Like most families, Nina and her husband had one child, a ten-year-old daughter. She shared the one bedroom with her grandmother while the lounge/dining room doubled as the parent's bedroom. Even with such a premium on space they had managed to cram a piano into the room, and they treated us to a mini-concert of classical Russian pieces. Scared stiff that we might be asked to respond, we offered our profound thanks and prepared to take our leave. Nina was shocked that we could even think of leaving before she had given each of us a gift. She scuttled off to various corners of the apartment and returned with a typical selection of Russian gifts that were handed out in turn. I was sitting at the end of the table and no gift remained for me. Nina gasped and motioned to us all to remain seated while she disappeared again. She reappeared triumphantly and, smiling apologetically, presented me with the only remaining gift she could find, a new pair of her husband's underpants. They were the wrong size for me, but I kept them in my wardrobe at home for years afterwards, feeling that it would somehow be a betrayal of trust to the wonderful Nina if I gave them away.

The most amazing selection of gifts were reserved for presentation at the final dinner in Kamenka before the BFC team were taken to catch the overnight train to Moscow. My own gift is still attached to the wall in the spare bedroom of my house. It's an enormous cuckoo clock. Unfortunately it makes such a noise that my family absolutely insisted that its mechanism be turned off because it was keeping everyone awake at night. The tick-tock alone was enough to wake the dead, but the sound of the cuckoo resembled the mating call of a hyena.

Dan's gift was an enormous wooden carving of an eagle with outstretched wings, about three feet high and almost as wide, rather resembling the statue of the 'Angel of the North' near Gateshead. It was only when we tried to board the train to Moscow, in a totally inebriated state and at the same time as exchanging emotional farewells with our hosts, that the true difficulty of transporting a life-size, wooden eagle became apparent. Dan, who had drunk every toast in vodka rather than adopting my cowardly approach of substituting mineral water whenever no one was looking, was holding the eagle in a warm embrace, while also carrying a suitcase and briefcase. He was wearing his new coat, but only after someone had actually remembered it on his behalf and physically put his arms through the sleeves.

With as much dignity as is possible when waltzing with an eagle, he crossed the platform and climbed the steps of the train, only to be catapulted back on to the platform because the width of the wings was greater than the width of the door. This pantomime was repeated on a number of occasions. It appeared not to occur to Dan that if he waltzed in sideways rather than making a full-frontal attack on each occasion he might have more luck. He resisted all attempts to take the eagle from him, saying it was the most wonderful present he had ever been given and he would never be parted from it. Eventually, our Russian hosts, wiping the tears from their eyes, and fearing that they might have Dan on extended loan, lifted him physically off his feet, still clutching the eagle to his bosom, turned him sideways and posted him through the door to be caught by various BFC team members on the other side. In this position they were both laid on a bunk and slept soundly all the way to Moscow.

I visited Russia several times over the following years, criss-crossing the country in night- sleeper trains with the door-handles tied with rope while we slept to keep out thieves (a blooming nuisance when you wanted to get up in the middle of the night for a pee). Even worse was travel on internal Aeroflot flights when I was often unnerved by the seemingly abortive attempts of the ground staff to de-ice the wings before take-off. I always studiously avoided Eddie's advice, given in Afghanistan many years before, to check the tread on the tyres before boarding, preferring my own 'ignorance is bliss' approach. I visited some dire industrial cities with no saving graces and the wonderful city of St. Petersburg, where my own cultural education was expanded out of all recognition. Mr Gorbachev (despised by every Russian I have ever met, in spite of his popularity abroad) gave way to the fascinating but chaotic regime of Mr Yeltsin, who later passed on the mantle of power to the Machiavellian Mr Putin.

Some visits took place in the heat of summer, when I learned that Russian mosquitoes, even in the Arctic Circle, are massively more of a nuisance than anywhere else in the world. I also visited in spring and autumn, each of which seemed to be over in the blink of an eye. But mostly I visited in winter because, somehow, it always seems to be winter in Russia. I bought a specially insulated coat from Berghaus to replace the ill-fitting sheepskin coat borrowed from a friend, but I was still cold. Along with others, I experienced the highs and lows of thinking that Russia was really on course for achieving a breakthrough in the transition to a market economy which would give better incomes to the people as a whole, and not just the new breed of gangster entrepreneurs, only to be downcast by the next piece of bad news, such as that one of our project interpreters in Togliatti had been murdered in a robbery. Or that a Russian manager of a wholesale market, who was about to come to the UK on a study tour organised by our company, would not be able to make it because somebody had lobbed a hand grenade into his office. The unfortunate man was sitting at his desk at the time. It is difficult to feel at ease in a country where these things happen, where you are advised not to open a project bank account because informers will pass on details of your name, address and bank balance to the men in sharp suits and sunglasses, or where your own project driver, on meeting you at the airport in Moscow, proudly displays his new possession to ensure your safety, kept in a paper bag in the glove compartment: a loaded gun.

We managed several projects in Russia which had varying degrees of success, some of them running for three or four years. The projects that worked best were those aimed at helping Russians to operate successful private companies in the food chain at the level of retail shops or wholesale markets. But projects at the level of the farm came up against the massive Russian conservatism over making any changes in the ownership of land or in rural life in general, even though that is where the need is often greatest. Most projects were financed and supervised by the European Union's TACIS programme, whose rating out of 10 for efficiency during this period I would put at 2. Little better was the British Government's Know How Fund. The best that can be said of all the projects run by these organisations is that they helped in the general process of showing that the outside world cared about what was going on in the old Eastern Bloc and helped to build a familiarity with how to run private businesses.

As for Dan, the last I heard of him he was going back to Russia with another company to advise on the restructuring of a processing plant. I hope he remembered his coat.

Apart from Russia, during the 1990s, I visited Ukraine on several occasions, Kazakhstan a few times and short trips to two more Former Soviet Union countries, Latvia and Armenia. There was also plenty of restructuring work in Eastern Europe and my company had a long-term project in Bulgaria, requiring regular visits on my part. The Middle East became a busy area for my consultancy company and my work visits included Syria, Saudi Arabia, Israel and Gaza. The travel was often exhausting, but I never tired of visiting new places wherever they were in the world.

My old stamping grounds in Africa almost disappeared from our project lists at this time although I did manage a short visit to Kenya, Malawi and Zimbabwe before I finished this type of work in the early 2000s. My new area of interest was work for a medical research charity concerned with blindness and visual impairment, involving a limited amount of travel to such wonderful places as Rio de Janeiro and Taiwan, but that's a different story.

Printed in Great Britain
by Amazon

67461471R00163